THE ROBOT'S DILEMMA

THEORETICAL ISSUES IN COGNITIVE SCIENCE

ZENON W. PYLYSHYN

University of Western Ontario
Series Editor

Language Learning and Concept Acquisition: Foundational Issues, William Demopoulos & Ausonio Marras, Editors (1986)

From Models to Modules: Studies in Cognitive Science from the McGill Workshops, Irwin Gopnik & Myrna Gopnik, Editors (1986)

Meaning and Cognitive Structure: Issues in the Computational Theory of Mind, Edited by Zenon W. Pylyshyn & William Demopoulos (1986)

The Robot's Dilemma: The Frame Problem in Artificial Intelligence, edited by Zenon W. Pylyshyn (1987)

THE
ROBOT'S
DILEMMA:

The Frame Problem in Artificial Intelligence

edited by
Zenon W. Pylyshyn
University of Western Ontario

ABLEX PUBLISHING CORPORATION
NORWOOD, NEW JERSEY

Second Printing 1988

Printed in the United States of America.

Library of Congress Cataloging-in-Publication Data

The Robot's dilemma.

  (Theoretical issues in cognitive science)
  Includes bibliographies and index.
  1. Artificial intelligence   I. Pylyshyn, Zenon W., 1937-   . II. Series.
Q355.R63   1986   006.3   86-22127
ISBN 0-89391-371-5

ABLEX Publishing Corporation
355 Chestnut Street
Norwood, New Jersey 07648

Contents

v

Preface

Zenon W. Pylyshyn

University of Western Ontario, Canada

There have been many worries over the years concerning the existence of deep problems that might prevent the realization of intelligent thinking machines. Most of these worries have turned out to be based either on a misunderstanding of the nature of computing and/or of intelligence or on some vague and ill-defined uneasiness associated with the recognition that automating intelligence appears to be very hard in practice. Neither of these sources of uneasiness is, in itself, a reason to worry: All scientific puzzles appear very difficult and complex until the right formulation is discovered.

Although it is widely recognized that building artificial intelligence machines with some significant generality is beyond the current scientific and technical horizon, there is very little understanding of where the major sources of difficulty lie. Though there has been a great deal of broad-brush speculation concerning this question (e.g., Dreyfus, 1979), much of it has missed its mark because of a lack of specificity as to the nature of the difficulties being raised. In fact, many of the strongest objections to AI have not been concerned with potential *performance* limitations, but rather with philosophical worries about whether machines could be truly said to *believe*, to *know*, to *mean*, to *understand* (e.g., Searle, 1980), to *feel*, and so on (see, e.g., the commentaries on Pylyshyn, 1978, or Pylyshyn, 1980). Thus when a real technical problem is raised which appears to have the makings of a serious difficulty that might prevent the realization of a high-performance general reasoning system, it is worth examining.

Such appears to be the case with a class of problems that might be referred to as problems of **holism** in reasoning. General reasoning—as opposed to reasoning about a closed topic area (such as, perhaps, chess)—requires that the cognitive system have the potential to connect any item of knowledge or belief (i.e., any representation) with any other. This is because cognition involves inference and inference can in principle lead from any belief **P** and any other belief **Q** by a chain of inferences to some consequence which *could* be relevant to the interpretation or understanding of some current situation. Thus, for example, in order to understand what the referent of the italicized pronoun is in sentences such as (1) below, arbitrary knowledge of the world has to be brought to bear. Moreover, there is no way to exclude any fact in advance as being irrelevant, without considering all implications of that fact; because there just could be some consequence at the end of a long chain of inferences that bore directly on the assignment of the anaphoric referent (see Pylyshyn, 1984, for more on this point).

(1) The city councillors refused to issue the workers a permit for a demonstration because *they* . . .

                              feared violence.
                              were communists.
                              were preparing for an election.
                              were from out of town.
                              applied too late.

The point is not that humans are able to draw all the consequences of their beliefs (they clearly can't), but that there appears to be no way *in general* to index beliefs so as to exclude certain obviously irrelevant paths of inference in advance, without at the same time excluding some obviously relevant ones. On the other hand, if "irrelevant" inference attempts are not suppressed, the cognitive system will become mired in an exponentially expanding range of inferences and will never be able to deal intelligently with domains requiring a potentially unbounded domain of knowledge— such as is involved in carrying on the simplest everyday conversation. Even in the case of large, finite domains the range of inferences increases exponentially with the number of facts the system knows. This is clearly an undesirable feature, since it does not appear that people take more time to make simple decisions about acts like reaching for the salt when they know more about, say, chemistry.

The general problem of holism is tantalizing, but one might still hope for a more technically well-defined "hard problem." Now there is a particular kind of holism problem that surfaced in AI a number of years ago, first described in a classical paper by McCarthy and Hayes (1969), which appeared to many people sufficiently precise that it could serve to focus the "holism" worry and could help cast some light on a deep puzzle of AI. This problem has become known as the *frame problem.* The name was chosen because it initially arose in connection with a particular formalism that was proposed for representing knowledge needed to reason about actions—a formalism which required statements ("axioms") that specified which properties of the world would remain unchanged when a certain action was carried out. The apparent need for such statements, called "frame axioms," presented a serious problem because there was no limit to how many of them might be required in a reasonably complex world, and hence to the number of inferences concerning non-change that would have to be made—after all, think of all the things in the world that *do not* change when you take a step across the room.

It soon became apparent, however, that examples such as those used to illustrate the frame problem (say, in the original McCarthy and Hayes [1969] paper, or later expository papers such as those by Raphael, 1971, or Simon, 1972) all harbored a deeper problem than that of finding a better representational formalism or a better modal logic. The type of examples discussed by most authors (both those working in Artificial Intelligence and those outside the field) who refer to the frame problem involves a certain difficulty encountered when a robot (or an organism) reasons about what might happen if it were to take a certain action. The problem arises because the range of things that change and those that do not change as a result of a certain action being taken cannot be specified in any simple manner in advance of any reasoning about the situation—which, as we have already remarked, can in principle involve any belief at all that the system holds. What I, or any intelligent robot, will conclude might result from a certain action being taken could depend on anything that I know about the world. For in principal *anything* can change as a result of my attempting to, say, pick up a cup. For example, I may know that there is a string attached to the cup which will initiate a chain of events culminating in the disappearance of the cup, or even the room. Because knowing what will change can depend on apparently unrelated facts—facts which are connected to the action in question by arbitrarily long chains of inference —it appears that a robot would have to carry out arbitrarily long chains of inferences, including inferences concerning what will *not* change, before it can take the simplest action (the essays by Janlert and by Dennett, this volume, give clear examples of this).

Although people do not consider all possibilities in planning ahead, neither do they simply consider beliefs that mention the action in question; i.e., they do not simply consider facts that can be indexed in advance as relevant to each action. If they did, they would make all sorts of obvious errors that they do not make. The problem is how to arrange for a mechanical system to (a) not make the most egregious and obvious errors, and (b) not get bogged down in an endless process of reasoning before taking any action (what Jerry Fodor, in his essay in this volume, calls "Hamlet's problem"). Another way to put this problem is to say that Artificial Intelligence must face the problem of determining the *relevance* of facts it knows to some problem at hand. This, the *problem of relevance*, is what many believe lies at the heart of the frame problem, and which will continue to be a serious problem long after all the minor technical problems (e.g., concerning the need for "frame axioms") have been dealt with.

Each of the essays that appears here devotes considerable space to defining and elaborating the notion of the frame problem—and the authors do this in a particularly cogent and entertaining manner. Hence it is inappropriate for me to devote space to that task in this introduction, beyond the brief sketch presented above. The papers appearing here have been brought together primarily through serendipity. It happened that a number of very interesting unpublished papers dealing with the frame problem crossed my desk a few years ago. My interest was spurred initially by papers written by Lars-Erik Janlert, Daniel Dennett[1], and Clark Glymour, as well as some remarks contained in Jerry Fodor's (1983) book, *Modularity of Mind*. This led me to make inquiries concerning the existence of other papers on the subject. In the process I discovered that a number of people, including John Haugeland, Hubert Dreyfus, and Patrick Hayes had independently been writing, or planning to write, on that topic. With their encouragement I asked Drew McDermott and Jerry Fodor to add their own perspectives. The result is this rather sharply focused discussion on one of the "hard problems" of artificial intelligence.

Because many of the authors had an opportunity to see papers written earlier by other authors, the discussion has also turned out to be a debate of sorts. Although some of the rhetoric gets quite heated in places—I should say more than I would have preferred—I believe the disputatious style not only helps to clarify the problem at hand, but also casts some light on the different approaches to an important challenge taken by people in artificial intelligence and by certain philosophers who have been concerned with related problems in their field. This book should therefore not be read merely as a discussion of the "frame problem" narrowly conceived, but also as a general analysis of what could be a major challenge to the design of computer systems exhibiting general intelligence.

---

[1] The essay by Dennett has since been published by Cambridge University Press (1984) in a collection entitled *Minds, Machines and Evolution* edited by Christopher Hookway. It is reproduced here by permission of the author, editor, and Cambridge University Press.

REFERENCES

Dreyfus, H.L. (1979). *What computers can't do: A critique of artificial reason.* 2nd ed. New York: Harper & Row.

Fodor, J.A. (1983). *The modularity of mind: An essay on faculty psychology.* Cambridge, MA: MIT Press, a Bradford Book.

McCarthy, J., & P. Hayes (1969). Some philosophical problems from the standpoint of artificial intelligence. In B. Meltzer & D. Michie (eds.), *Machine intelligence 4.* Edinburgh: Edinburgh University Press.

Pylyshyn, Z.W. (1978). Computational models and empirical constraints. *Behavioral and Brain Sciences, 1,* 93–99.

Pylyshyn, Z.W. (1980). Cognition and computation: Issues in the foundations of cognitive science. *Behavioral and Brain Sciences, 3*(1), 111–132.

Pylyshyn, Z.W. (1984). *Computation and cognition: Toward a foundation for cognitive science.* Cambridge, MA: MIT Press, a Bradford Book.

Raphael, B. (1971). The frame problem in problem-solving systems. In N.V. Findler & B. Meltzer (Eds.), *Artificial intelligence and heuristic programming* (pp. 159–169). Edinburgh: Edinburgh University Press.

Searle, J. (1980). Minds, brains, and programs. *Behavioral and Brain Sciences, 3*(3) 417–457.

Simon, H.A. (1972). On reasoning about actions. In H.A. Simon & L. Siklossy (Eds.), *Representation and meaning: Experiments with information processing systems* (pp. 414–430). Englewood Cliffs, NJ: Prentice-Hall.

CHAPTER 1

Modeling Change—
The Frame Problem

Lars-Erik Janlert

University of Umeå, Sweden

AI has with few exceptions overlooked the importance of metaphysical deliberations. One consequence of this neglect is the repeated failure to solve the frame problem.

PART 1: DEFINING THE PROBLEM

This is an attempt to elucidate the so-called *frame problem* in Artificial Intelligence, roughly the problem of representing change. On the basis of an examination of suggested solutions to the frame problem, which makes up the main bulk of this paper, it appears safe to claim that the frame problem has not yet been solved. And, I regret to say, there is nothing like a complete solution to be found in this paper either. What I have to offer is a more definite notion of what the frame problem *is*, what would constitute a solution to it, and an indication of the general direction in which a solution should be sought.

The major part of this paper was written while I was a research associate on the project *Modeling Time* at the Departments of Linguistics and Information Processing, University of Umeå, supported by the Swedish Humanities and Social Sciences Research Council (HSFR), 79/80–81/81.

Bo Dahlbom has criticized, encouraged, and helped me in various ways through several versions of this paper, I have also received valuable support and comments from Eva Ejerhed, Axel Ruhe, Martin Edman, Peter Gärdenfors, Kenneth Kahn, Staffan Löf, Zenon Pylyshyn, Ingemar Widegren, and others.

Part 1 sets the stage for the critical survey in Part 2. First, the original frame problem is introduced and put into a historical perspective. The *general* frame problem is then defined as the problem of finding a representational form permitting a changing, complex world to be efficiently and adequately represented. This definition permits us to single out the frame problem from a cluster of related problems: the prediction problem, the revision problem, the qualification problem, and the general bookkeeping problem.

Part 2 contains the survey of solution attempts: frames, causal connection, consistency, STRIPS, PLANNER, Unless, TMS, and a few other related ideas.

Part 3 sums up the examination by discussing some important points and by drawing some general conclusions: McCarthy's situation concept is an inappropriate basis for a metaphysics of change; the frame problem is the problem to find the metaphysics of the modeled world and make it the metaphysics of the modeling system, which requires the metaphysics to be intrinsically represented.

Representation and Problem Solving

The frame problem is a *general* problem of representation, relevant to all types of setups where a complex and changing world is to be represented. Historically, the frame problem is intimately linked to the research on problem solving and planning[1] in AI—a research that has as one of its most basic assumptions that the problem solver should have at its disposal an internal symbolic model or representation of the problem world. By manipulations on this internal model, corresponding to real-world actions, the problem solver can do such things as predict what would happen if a certain action were performed, decide which conditions must be fulfilled to be able to produce a particular situation, compare different hypothetical states of affairs, etc.

This idea of internal representation is brought out clearly in a distinction between *epistemology*[2] and *heuristics*, introduced by John McCarthy and Patrick Hayes (1969), that has been generally adopted in AI under various aliases. The epistemological component of the problem solver models the world, and the heuristic component does the problem solving (the talk about *components* should not be taken too literally).

Unfortunately, these concepts are far from clear and well understood. Basically, epistemology is the penultimate[3] arbiter of plans proposed by

---

[1] Here, *problem solving* is used as a general term, including *planning*—solving problems of achieving a certain state of affairs by actions—as a special case.

[2] Readers with a background in philosophy had better not think of the usual connotations of the term.

[3] The *ultimate* arbiter is, of course, reality.

the heuristics; it is what it takes to determine if a proposed plan stands a good chance of succeeding. Contrasting with this *selective* role of the epistemology is heuristics as a *generator* of plans. As the name implies, we certainly expect it to be a *smart* generator—something considerably better than exhaustive search. In practice, processes of generation and selection are intricately interwoven, which makes the distinction difficult to apply. Our understanding of the distinction between epistemology and heuristics also involves a range of more or less loosely associated ideas: justification vs. discovery, certainty vs. uncertainty, deduction vs. induction, knowledge vs. reasoning, neutral vs. goal directed, reason vs. will, etc. Disentangling all this would require a separate study. I will simply proceed on the assumption that we have a general idea of what epistemology and heuristics are, which will do for the present purpose.

It is tempting to speculate on a general trade-off between modeling and heuristics. Some problem solvers may rely on having a very rich and accurate model of the world, and then they don't have to be very clever, because all they have to do is to consult the model for the answers. But some problem solvers may rely on their cleverness—what they don't know they can always figure out—and so manage without much explicit knowledge of the world.

The research on mechanical problem solving can be roughly classified as belonging to two different research traditions: a deductivist and a non-deductivist. Although there has been an exchange of ideas and techniques between them, each tradition has preserved its own view on the problem of problem solving and how it should be attacked; for example, deductivists have a particular concern for modeling (epistemology), whereas non-deductivists have a particular concern for heuristics.

The Non-Deductive Approach

The non-deductivist tradition is the older of the two. It has its roots in a psychologically oriented approach to artificial intelligence that assumes that the most practicable road to artificial intelligence systems is via the study and imitation of natural intelligence. On this view the intelligent machine simulates the brain at a high level, in terms of *thoughts, reasoning*, etc.

Human reasoning does not seem to depend very much on deductive inferences, at least not at the level of reasoning which Allen Newell and Herbert Simon have explored and documented in their *Human Problem Solving* (1972). The General Problem Solver (GPS) of Newell, Shaw, and Simon (1960) uses not logic and deduction, but a *means–ends analysis* for its reasoning. Here is a much-simplified description of how it works: The goal is approached in a series of steps. Each step starts with calculating the difference between what has been achieved so far and the goal. On the basis of the characteristics of this difference, operations that are most likely to have an effect in reducing the difference are tried in succession until an operation succeeds in bringing the system closer to its goal.[4] The reasoning that takes place in the process of solving a problem is mainly heuristic: It is by informed guesses, rules of thumb, trial and error, etc, that a solution is reached.

Some systems, although non-deductivist in spirit, depend considerably on deductive methods. A notable example is STRIPS (Fikes & Nilsson, 1971). In STRIPS, reasoning *within* a given world–state or *situation* (see below) proceeds deductively and is sharply distinguished from reasoning *between* different world–states, which proceeds in a GPS-like manner. These two modes of reasoning—within a given world–state, and between different world–states—I will call *synchronic* and *diachronic,* respectively. Diachronic reasoning is of course crucial to the system's planning ability, which is why I don't hesitate to place STRIPS within the non-deductivist tradition. In fact, STRIPS was introduced as a system that liberated dia-chronic reasoning from deductivistic constraints (at the time, the deduct-ivist tradition was dominating), and thereby, it was contended, solved the frame problem.

The Deductive Approach

In approaching the problem of problem solving, free from psychological considerations and inspirations—either because of a technological, perfor-mance-oriented outlook, or because one has in view to study *intelligence per se* (one variety of which happens to be instantiated in humans)—*logic* stands out as a promising means for implementing symbolic models of problem–worlds. Logic is a formal language with well-understood syntax and semantics, which should make it suitable for machine application. Furthermore, it comes with a deductive system, a mechanism of inference. The deductive structure, however, could not be put to practical use until the *resolution method* was formulated (Robinson, 1965), a method that made it feasible to construct logical proofs mechanically. It soon turned out to be possible to use formal logic and mechanical theorem provers to implement question-answering systems (synchronic reasoning), and even more general problem-solving systems. The ensuing deductively oriented research in AI can boast of a solid and prestigious basis in the long and suc-cessful history of deductive ideals in Western philosophy and science.

The efficiency of pure theorem provers in solving general problems is often unacceptably low—considerable amounts of more or less domain-specific heuristics are needed to make a deductively based system work

---

[4] The feedback mechanisms studied by early cybernetics were quantitative and continu-ous. GPS can be seen as a qualitative and discrete feedback system.

reasonably well. Nevertheless, the deductivist tradition attaches greater weight to the problem solver's ability to model the world, its epistemological power. Difficulties are met with a general strategy of extending the ontology, to include for example history, intentions, and knowledge as entities in the model explicit to the system itself. Extensions of logic itself are rare—there seems to be a general conviction within the deductivist tradition that a fairly simple logic will do, preferably first-order, predicate logic. (An exception is the recent, not wholly successful, attempt to develop a non-monotonic logic; see Part 2 below.)

A central concept of the deductivist paradigm, which is rather popular also with non-deductivists, is the *situation*, "the complete state of affairs at some instant of time" (McCarthy, 1968, p. 411). The world is conceived as a sequence of situations, determined by a set of *laws of motion*. A description of a situation consists of a set of sentences of first-order logic.[5] The deductive system can then be used to infer other sentences which also apply to the same situation. Explicit knowledge is in this way complemented by implicit knowledge, by means of synchronic reasoning. Moreover, *physical determinism* is assumed: "The laws of motion of a system determine all future situations from a given situation" (McCarthy, 1968, p. 411). That is, given the laws of motion, a description of a situation, and an action, a description of the new situation that would result if the action was executed can be deductively inferred. Thus, also diachronic reasoning is deductive.

A summary of some important ideas in the original deductivist setting follows:

1. The situation concept of McCarthy and the related concepts of action and law of motion.
2. The use of first-order logic to represent situations.
3. The use of first-order logic to represent laws of motion. Deductive relations between descriptions of situations: physical determinism.
4. Actions are the only entities that have the power to create a new situation. Nothing happens that is not caused by an action.
5. The problem solver is the only agent; all actions are actions of the problem solver.
6. When an action is performed the problem world reaches a new equilibrium fast. A new action is never initiated before the commotion caused by the preceding action has petered out.
7. There is no history in the situations—there is no explicit memory of past actions, no objects or properties designed to represent earlier events.

---

[5] A caveat: I will frequently write *situation* when I mean a description of the situation, *action* when I mean the action's representation in the problem-solving system, etc.

8.   The problem world is in principle completely described. The effects of an action on every detail of the problem world is completely specified.

Several of these points are apparently consequences of a decision to avoid interfering processes—there is to be no explicit treatment of interactions. There are no other agents whose actions may interfere with the problem solver's own actions, and an action is not allowed to interfere with previous actions. Causal chains are not explicitly represented. Since there are no simultaneous events, nor memory of past events, it appears more expedient to deduce all effects of an action at once, skipping intermediate results.

In short: the early deductivists were committed to a simplified seventeenth-century mechanics way of representing the world.

The Original Frame Problem

The deductive research program soon ran into difficulties. In the process of formulating laws of motion it turned out that the relevant laws were drowned in a flood of seemingly irrelevant but necessary *pseudolaws*. Deducing a new situation requires not only that changes effected by an action are inferable, but also that what *does not* change can be inferred. And, in fact, *very little* of what from a purely logical point of view could happen as a result of an action, does happen. Whereas it is logically possible that turning on the light in my living room will make the walls turn black, halt inflation, and raise the melting point of lead, nothing of this does in fact happen. Every empirical truth relevant to the modeling task has to be imposed on the logic in the form of proper axioms.

The outcome is a problem solver sitting in the midst of a sea of axioms representing non-changes, endlessly calculating non-effects. This is *the frame problem* in its original manifestation; let us look at some details.

A sentence which is true of one situation may be false of another. Somehow each sentence in the model must be tagged with the situation to which it applies. One way of doing that is McCarthy's *fluent*. For example, *rain(x)* is a fluent such that rains(x)[s] is true if, and only if, it rains at x in the situation s.

Let us illustrate with an example from the *blocks–world*—a toy world containing some blocks on a table and a robot hand that can do things such as move to different positions, grasp a block, etc. The GRASP-operation could be defined by the following law of motion (using fluents):

$$\forall s \forall x \forall y \, ((\text{HAND-OVER}(x) \wedge \text{HAND-FREE} \wedge \text{BLOCK}(x) \wedge \text{ON}(x,y)) \, [s]$$
$$\rightarrow (\text{HOLDS}(x) \wedge \text{HAND-OVER}(y)) [\text{GRASP}[s]])$$

That is: If the hand is over x (in the situation s) and it is empty (in s) and x is a block (in s) and x is on y (in s); then the operation GRASP will result in a situation GRASP[s] where the hand is holding x and is above y. This is all that can be said of the new situation, given this law. Note that ON(x,y) is no longer known to be true (neither is it known to be false), and that the hand is no longer known to be free (and neither is it known not to be free). If we want x to remain a block, that fact must be possible to infer, for example by including BLOCK(x) in the consequent of the implication. If we do not want the other blocks to lose their existence or properties, all these facts must also be explicitly included in the laws of motion. Everything that does not change has to be included.

Normally these non-changes are represented by special axioms, so-called *frame axioms*. A frame axiom for GRASP might be:

∀s∀x (BLOCK(x)[s]⊃BLOCK(x)[GRASP[s]])

These axioms represent the frame of reference for the action, that is, the background that remains unaffected (hence the name *frame problem*). Clearly, this way of modeling is not practicable in a slightly more complex problem world; the frame axioms will occupy all space and the deductions of non-changes, all time.

The General Frame Problem

At this point one may begin to suspect that the frame problem is really just a consequence of choosing *logic* as the representation language. Will the problem not simply disappear if we abandon the strict use of logic? For example, we could try to introduce some kind of convention that things not explicitly changed are taken to be unchanged.

Superficially, this would seem to solve the problem. Unfortunately, only superficially—new problems crop up that are, like the original frame problem, intimately connected with the *phenomenon of change*. As we shall see in Part 2, the attacks on the frame problem have so far resulted in little more than pushing it around and rephrasing it in various ways. It is now widely accepted that the original frame problem is just one manifestation of a *general* and—some would say—*profound* problem of dealing with change. It is the *frame problem* in this *general* sense I address in this paper. Whether there is a general *solution* is a much more controversial matter.

The frame problem is not just a minor technical nuisance, but a very real and serious obstacle to the design of any kind of system that is to model a complex and changing world. While anticipating the analysis and discussion that follow, here is my definition of the problem. *The general frame problem* is the problem of finding a representational form permitting a changing, complex world to be efficiently and adequately represented. There are three points in particular to which I wish to draw attention:

1. *The frame problem is a problem of modeling, not of heuristics.* For one thing, because the problem solver will not always know in advance what it will do next, that requires a good understanding of the present situation also in aspects not directly addressed in its previous problem-solving activities. Second, because the frame problem is real enough, even if we don't set out to make a *problem-solving* system.

2. *The frame problem is not a question of content, but of form.* Logic is perfectly capable of representing the blocks–world, as far as *content* is concerned. The frame problem is an indication that *informationally equivalent systems,* systems conveying the same information about the represented world, may yet differ *drastically* in *efficiency.* The situation is somewhat analogous to choosing between different programming languages; although they are computationally equivalent in the mathematical sense, we recognize that there are important differences in the ease and efficiency with which they are applied to different types of tasks.

3. *The choice of suitable form depends on the problem world—computational considerations will not suffice.* The frame problem is not strictly a problem of inventing the right data structures and algorithms from an internal computer-science perspective; its solution requires that we seriously take into account how the problem world fundamentally is.

We should expect that there was a frame problem also in the early non-deductivist systems, such as GPS. But the circumstances were not such that the frame problem could crystallize into a problem separable from general bookkeeping problems; modeling was not very developed nor clearly distinguished from heuristics, and there was a mathematically inspired tendency to view actions as complete transformations of the world rather than piecemeal manipulations. In the deductively based systems the frame problem is so much more conspicuous, which makes the deductivist research tradition's ideas and views the natural point of departure for discussing the frame problem.

The frame problem is one of four closely related, and sometimes confused, problems pertaining to the modeling of change. The other three are: (a) the prediction problem (Hayes, 1971), (b) the bookkeeping problem, and (c) the so-called qualification problem (McCarthy, 1980). By showing what the frame problem is *not*, I hope to give it a more distinct demarcation. I will argue that the frame problem, the prediction problem, and the bookkeeping problem concern, respectively, the metaphysical, the instrumental, and the implementational adequacy of the representation. The qualification problem can be construed as the problem of applying idealized knowledge to the real world, involving the frame problem as well as the prediction problem.

The Prediction Problem

Sometimes a prediction does not come true; a certain sequence of operations has been calculated to solve a certain problem, but when the plan is executed it somehow fails to accomplish its goal. This may happen even if we disregard the possibility of mistakes due to carelessness, forgetfulness, and the like—errors that a mechanical problem solver is not likely to be prone to. Given the laws of motion and a description of a real-world situation it is still possible that a correct application of the laws to the given description will produce a prediction that does not completely agree with the subsequent real-world situation. In such a case, either the laws or the description of the given situation must be imperfect.

In practice, this is an inevitable difficulty. We have to accept that predictions can go wrong, and in fact in non-trivial systems it will happen frequently enough to warrant the introduction of some mechanism of revision whereby the system may automatically correct itself. The *revision problem* is concerned with the construction of such mechanisms. I will come back to it at the end of this section.

The nature of the prediction problem can be uncovered by discussing some important factors that limit the system's ability to make correct predictions. To start with, the principle of determinism may itself be put in question; as we move to more complex problem–worlds, for example, including conversation with humans, one may begin to doubt that there really exists a totally determining set of laws. For the sake of argument, however, determinism is assumed in the following.

Let us make a distinction between the system's point of view and the outside observer's point of view. As an extreme case, consider a system that from the outside point of view totally lacks perception. The system may yet consistently believe that it makes authentic observations of the world and find itself always in complete agreement with its reality, given laws and descriptions that produce descriptions constituting what the outside observer considers to be its self-generated perceptions. So this is one way, admittedly weird, of "solving" the prediction problem: by isolating the system from the world, letting it withdraw to a hallucinatory world controlled only by itself. Obviously, we have only theoretical use of such systems.

From the outside observer's point of view there are some limitations in the modeling that have a negative effect on the reliability of predictions. McCarthy (1968, p. 411) says that a representation of a situation is necessarily only partial. The scope of a representation is for practical reasons limited. But perfectly isolated parts of the world are rare, if they exist at all. Anyway, a part of the world that *appears* isolated to the system, and that includes everything more directly relevant to the problem at hand, will most likely be far too large to represent *in toto*. Thus, the limit in scope limits the reliability of predictions.

Given a particular language or form of representation, a description expressed in this language remains ambiguous even if it says all that can be truthfully said using this language. At least, there is a widespread *belief* that the world always exceeds any description of it in richness of details and subtlety of nuances. And, of course, if the system has only one concept of red, for example, it will not be able to discriminate between different nuances of red, so its description of some red object will be satisfied by several possible situations. From the outside point of view, the system divides the world into equivalence–classes, each class appearing to the system as a unique situation. As far as the prediction problem is concerned, this may seem unimportant; a coarse description can be quite as truthful as a more detailed description, and we have some freedom to choose the level of detail to fit our purpose. However, a coarse-grained representation may have unpleasant side effects: There will possibly be, from the system's point of view, unobservable, unrepresentable processes at work underground that now and then will surprise the system by producing perceivable effects that the system cannot anticipate. To guarantee accurate predictions at a coarse level of description, we may be forced to use forms of representations that are too fine grained and too resource demanding, to be practically feasible.

Incidentally, this suggests another "solution" to the prediction problem: making the system so dull and undiscriminating that its predictions run very little risk of being wrong. Such a system is like the perception-free system in that it becomes isolated from the world—as the number of world-states it can differentiate between diminishes, it loses contact with reality.

The coarseness of the representation language may be countered by introducing an idealized problem world (there might of course also be other reasons for doing this) which exactly matches the resolving power of the language. In an idealized world we could, for example, limit the repertoire of red colors to just one. Evidently, as soon as we apply calculated solutions of problems in the idealized world to the real world, we run into a new source of inaccuracy: the discrepancy between the idealized world and the real world. The early research in mechanical problem solving was inclined to use extremely idealized problem worlds, like the blocks-world. In these neat and tidy environments the efforts could be concentrated on pure problem solving. Some of these idealized problem worlds make possible systems that have completely accurate representations (of the idealized world, that is), systems that in fact do not suffer from the prediction problem. This "solution" of the prediction problem is yet another version of the perception-free, hallucinating system.

For various reasons, descriptions are commonly less than total even when considered from the system's point of view. One obvious reason is incomplete perception: hidden views, etc. Another common reason is that goals are seldom totally specified, partly because the system wants to solve a *class* of problems, partly for reasons of economy and focus of interest; there may be a specific interest in having block A on top of block B, without caring the least what happens to block D. Notice also that a more fully specified goal runs a greater risk of being impossible to attain. There may also be actions with less than total specificity (see Part 2: Unless, below), reducing the degree of specification. With these observations we have approached the last important limiting factor that will be discussed here.

The best map is not the terrain itself. The more minutely we represent the world, the more complex the representation, till at last it is too complex to be useful. As an extreme, consider the case where the more exact method of representation is so slow as to produce the correct prediction at a time when the predicted situation already has occurred. Painstaking precautions to avoid mistakes are not always worthwhile. This is a point where trying to cope with the frame problem appears to be at odds with solving the prediction problem. Most probably there are such conflicts, but the problem of mastering complexity is a more general concern than the frame problem. Even in systems modeling static worlds we may have to simplify in order to make problem solving and question answering reasonably efficient.

In all these cases, imperfect prediction calls for readjustment and revision of the model after failures. The task of finding good strategies for revision might be called the *revision problem*. I think it is important to keep a distinction between revision and debugging. *Debugging* is something that takes place between the heuristics and the epistemology, when the epistemology isn't quite satisfied with what the heuristics has come up with.[6] Debugging implies an investigation into *how* the system has come to have a faulty belief.

Revision, on the other hand, is the concern of some basic support system for the model. Primarily, it is just a way to get rid of conflicting facts as fast and painlessly as possible; readjusting to new, unexpected, circum-

---

[6] Of course, the term "debug" reflects only *one* type of idea about how to exploit discarded plans; a good plan is a bad plan minus a number of errors. Incidently, the term *debugging*, as used for developing general plans or acquiring general laws, suggests an inductive or cumulative view: The laws are essentially correct; they just need yet some small adjustments to work perfectly.

stances with a minimum effort and a minimum loss of information. The purpose of revision is thus *not* to make appropriate "corrections" so that future predictions will be more accurate. The discussion above points out the limits of such refinements; besides, adjusting to the unexpected, and learning from it, are not in general the same.

It should be clear at this point that the prediction problem and the frame problem are distinct; recall that it was in the very same early problem-solving systems, that had actually eliminated the prediction problem by using idealized problem–worlds, that the frame problem was first discovered. To sum up: The prediction problem is the problem of making the representation *instrumentally* adequate; it is mainly the problem of representing the *physics* of the modeled world. It explicitly does not concern the *form* or the *internal workings* of the representation. *That*, precisely, is what the *frame problem* is about: to choose a form of representation that makes for efficient administration, a form in which the physics is efficiently *expressed*. In particular I will suggest that the suitable form is determined by the *metaphysics* of the modeled world, so we might say that the frame problem is mainly the problem of representing the *metaphysics* of the modeled world.

The General Bookkeeping Problem

The bookkeeping problem is the problem of keeping track of the various plans and hypothetical situations that the system, partly in parallel, makes use of during the planning process. One of the major problems is to simultaneously keep in storage several different descriptions of situations. There is also the problem of relating the descriptions to one another, for example that situation B is the calculated result of performing X in situation A. Various context mechanisms have been used to avoid duplications of information and to structure the set of situations.

On the face of it, the frame problem looks like a special case of a general, and rather fuzzy, bookkeeping problem. To be sure, they are both concerned with *efficient model administration*, but actually they have radically different characters. Most of all, it is a difference of approach. The bookkeeping problem implies an essentially technical view on the problem of representing change; an instrumentalist approach that opens up for patching and hacking. By now, it is rather evident that there is more needed than a bag of tricks to speed up and save space, a tactic somewhat reminiscent of a novice programmer trying hard to optimize the code instead of trying to find a better algorithm. A radical solution to bookkeeping problems requires a penetration in depth to the underlying causes of poor bookkeeping.

The frame problem, viewed as first and foremost a problem of *representation*—not administration, in particular the problem of representing the metaphysics—is one such in-depth approach. It invites to realism and theorizing, which I believe will be more fruitful in the development of more efficient methods for bookkeeping than direct attacks on the bookkeeping problems.

From this point of view, the bookkeeping problem is less a research problem than a *symptom* of deeper problems, one of which is the frame problem. But there is a genuine problem half hidden in the all-embracing worries about efficiency, which is: Assuming that we have found out what the representation should look like, how do we implement it? We have no reason to expect that there is a predestined perfect harmony between existing software and hardware, and the representational forms demanded (by the metaphysics, say).

I don't know if "the bookkeeping problem" is the most accurate heading for this, but I think that the most scientifically and technically interesting side of bookkeeping is the question of implementational adequacy, the question of how the adequately designed representational system is to be implemented using current hardware and software technology; or, if that can't be done, how we are to develop the required programming languages, computer architectures, hardware components, etc. Even if the instrumental sufficiency, the representational power, of our most cherished forms or languages of representation that are machine implemented, is not called in question, it just *may* be too hasty to assume that the demands on form and organization, raised by (for example) the frame problem, can be met with current hardware and software technology.

The Qualification Problem

A complete representation of all conditions that must be satisfied to guarantee a successful performance of an action puts an unreasonable, maybe unlimited, amount of qualifications on the laws defining the action. Here is an example from McCarthy (1980). The successful use of a rowboat to cross a river requires that the oars and rowlocks be present and unbroken, and that they fit each other. Many other qualifications can be added: The boat must be sufficiently watertight, it must have sufficient carrying capacity, there should be no logs floating in the river that could upset the boat, and so on—we have no trouble in extending the list indefinitely, it seems. The rules for using the boat rapidly become hopelessly complex to use.

This may seem to be the prediction problem seen from a different angle: How can we possibly account for all the premises that are needed to make safe predictions? We generally cannot. There *is no* fail-proof *closed formula* for crossing a real river by a real rowboat. Basically, this is why we need a model on which to "run" proposed plans. As far as the qualification problem *is* a problem it seems to be a problem of heuristics.

Yet, the qualification problem appears to bear on the frame problem as well. In fact, the qualification problem seems to involve epistemologically relevant decisions as to what properties of an object or an action are taken to be essential, which is a metaphysical question if any. Is it part of the essence of a rowboat that rowlocks be present? That the rowlocks be unbroken? Is it part of the essence of the MOVE-operation that what is to be moved is moveable? Etcetera.

I think that the qualification problem is largely just another way of expressing the problem of applying an idealized representation to the real world. In a commonsense type of idealized world there might, for example, be a law that says, without qualifications, that one can use a rowboat to cross a river. The epistemologically relevant part of the qualification problem is to apply that knowledge in a real situation: What qualifies as a rowboat (oars, watertight, etc.)? What qualifies as a river, etc.? Since one would expect an idealized world to differ from the real world both in its physics and its metaphysics, it would seem to explain why both the prediction problem and the frame problem are reflected in the qualification problem.

PART 2: SURVEY OF SUGGESTED SOLUTIONS

Frames

An event will normally affect the world only in a very limited aspect. Change of location does not affect colors. Painting does not change the location of things. Applying insecticides does not (at least, should not) affect the health of animals other than insects. If it were possible to separate the world into different aspects, so that the effects of a certain type of event are limited to a certain aspect associated with that particular type of event, it would follow that the world remains unchanged in every other aspect. This is the idea of *frames*, briefly discussed in McCarthy and Hayes (1969) and Hayes (1971, 1973).

A frame separates the description of the world into blocks, each corresponding to a different *aspect* of the world, so that an event belonging to a certain block affects only facts within the same block.[7] A new inference rule is introduced: If F is a formula true in situation s, the event e has the property of belonging to block j, and all nonlogical symbols crucially occurring in F belong to other blocks than j, then F remains true of the situation that results if the event e takes place in situation s. There are some

---

[7] The intention of Hayes (1971) and McCarthy and Hayes (1969) seems to be that the blocks are to be disjunct, but Hayes (1973) does not postulate this, and it is doubtful whether it is possible in a common sense world to have disjunct blocks.

choices as to the exact meaning of *crucially occur*, but the important point is that it remains a purely syntactically defined relation.

To carry out these ideas it will be necessary to cut the description of a situation into small pieces, where each piece belongs to a particular block. The reason is that we do not want an aggregation of information (e.g., a sentence) to be put in doubt in its entirety just because one of its parts belongs to the block that includes the current event. Block membership has to be decidable without knowledge of the context, i.e., the membership of a particular fact of a particular block must be independent of the other facts. This leads to a separation into blocks that is based on which predicates, functions, constants, etc., occur in the description.

The weak point in the frame idea is that the separation into blocks will have to be so coarse that it will be of little help. Even if we know that *painting* only affects the *color* block, we are still left with the considerable task of deciding exactly which of our facts involving color remain valid. If we stick to *natural* actions like *painting, moving*, and so on, the number of blocks has to be small; consequently, the average block has to be large. This follows from the inherent generality of natural actions. Any finer classification into many, smaller, blocks would only be disrupted by actions cutting across block boundaries. On the other hand, if we try to make a finer classification by reducing the natural actions into small atomic actions that affect the world in fewer aspects, we are confronted with three problems: (a) Natural actions have no fixed decomposition into atomic actions; there are, for example, innumerable ways of *moving* something; (b) instead of affecting one big block, the original action will now affect many small blocks, so the amount of work in deciding which facts have been changed is not necessarily reduced; and (c) it is doubtful whether the blocks in such a classification would have even the remotest affinity with *natural* aspects and *natural* commonsense properties.[8]

As an example of two blocks in a coarse but safe classification, Hayes mentions location and color. But consider a chameleon: Moving it will frequently incur a change in color. What affects what is apparently highly dependent on the circumstances, the particular environment of the events. As pointed out in McCarthy and Hayes (1969), it is not possible to make a classification into blocks that will apply always, in any environment. It is not even possible for a relatively limited part of the real world. This observation naturally leads to the idea of having many frames, each tailored to a particular kind of environment or activity. Thus specialized, the frame method would perform much better, allowing more reliable, as well as finer, classifications. We have now come quite close to the frame concept

---

[8] But why is it important to have *natural* actions, *natural* objects, *natural* properties, and so on? Are we really restricted to common sense metaphysics? I shall attempt an answer in Part 3.

of Minsky (1974), and the idea of prototype situations and environments. The price we have to pay is a new set of difficult problems. Among them is the problem of how and when to switch frames, and in this process, how to reshuffle information from the old frame into the blocks of the new frame. These problems remain largely unsolved. Add to this the disquieting question of how severe are the restrictions the general use of prototypes puts on the ability to model the world.

Causal Connection

There is a certain similarity between the method of frames, considered as an exploitation of the idea that the effects of an event are propagated *propertywise*—for example, painting affects a definite property of things, namely their color—and the method of causal connection (Hayes, 1971), which can be viewed as an attempt to formalize the idea that effects are propagated *objectwise*—painting affects things in the vicinity, movement within a room affects things in that room, etc.

A formal relation called *causal connection* is introduced that relates objects to each other, and also actions to objects, in a situation. Informally, that A is causally connected to B means that a change of some property of object B may cause a change of some property of object A. This relation is, according to Hayes, reflexive and transitive. If, in a given situation, it can be proved that an action and an object are not causally related, it is a valid inference that that object is not changed by the action.

The method of frames and the method of causal connection have a common strategy for the frame problem: giving general rules for classifying the different parts of a description into a class of facts that remain unchanged, and a class of facts that are candidates for being retracted or revised. In both methods, the strategy, even when successful, leaves us with a *local frame problem:* to decide what is, and what is not, changed within the class of doubtful facts. Notice that the causal connection relation depends on the situation. Contrary to the methods of frames where class membership is static, the method of causal connection allows dynamically varying membership; actions may establish new causal connections and remove old connections. This also allows for a flexible way of adding to the problem world, introducing additional mediate effects of the actions without having to redefine existing actions; the immediate effects could stay the same.[9]

We recall from the previous section that in the method of frames the local frame problem is in fact not very local. The method of causal connec-

---

[9] It seems reasonable that this is a condition that any solution to the frame problem must satisfy: that (conservative) additions to the problem–world do not require a complete recompilation of the model.

tion has a local frame problem that is probably even worse: The objects which are causally connected to the current action may change in every respect, not only in the property in virtue of which the causal connection holds. If, for example, a change of position of object A may cause a change of temperature in object B, the problem is to decide whether the temperature of B actually changes, plus the problem of deciding whether its color changes, its weight, electric potential, etc., change.

The usefulness of Hayes's proposal depends on whether it is in general possible to limit the causal connections of an action, indirect connections included, to a small number of objects. Unfortunately, there are causal connections (in Hayes's sense) that are almost ubiquitous. One example: Whenever two objects are in contact, or very close to each other, it is in general true that a change of position of one of the objects may cause a change of position in the other. The transitivity of the causal connections makes it plausible that most of the objects in an ordinary living room, say, are causally connected to each other. Furthermore, the causal connection relation does not discriminate between different types of causes so that *missing links* in the causal chains corresponding to, for example, change of temperature as a cause, will by transitivity probably be bridged by some other cause or causes.

For a particular problem it might in some cases be possible to keep down the number of causal connections by using a specially tailored representation.[10] Of course, such ad-hoc methods have very little to do with a general solution to the frame problem.

Consistency

The world is essentially inert. Things are generally inert; their properties are changed only exceptionally. Therefore, assume that each object retains its properties as long as this assumption does not lead to a contradiction. This view underlies the consistency-based methods for the frame problem. Surprisingly, the principle of inertness is not the motive stated in the introduction of the method (Hayes, 1973). Instead, the proposal is motivated by fears that the comprehensive axiom systems demanded by nontrivial problems will, in practice, contain inconsistencies and so be useless.

---

[10] The fact that Hayes's (1971) example, *the monkey and the bananas,* works at all, is completely dependent on that kind of move. For example, the function *location* is introduced as a loose horizontal coordinate measure together with an axiom to the effect that two objects are causally connected only if they have the same location. The axiom is misleadingly interpreted by Hayes as the principle that "there is no causality at a distance," which sounds like a well-known and respectable mechanistic principle—there can be no immediate action at a distance—but in fact the axiom forbids any causal chain extending beyond the location of the action. The result is a universe of completely isolated cells, each corresponding to a different location.

The method in short: Given a situation and an event we may, using the laws of motion, immediately infer certain changes giving us a partial description of the new situation. This partial description is completed by transferring the old description piece by piece under constant surveillance of the consistency of the new description being created, stopping when inconsistency arises. The task is to determine a maximal consistent description that extends the explicitly inferred partial description into the description of the old situation.

There are, as remarked by Hayes, two serious theoretical problems. First, consistency is not decidable for first-order theories. Second, there will generally be many maximal consistent extensions—which one should we choose, and why? The first problem is very serious to a deductivist since the deductivist ideal demands that inferences always are logically valid. Besides, it would seem to dispose of Hayes's original motivation for his proposal. By abandoning these ideals, ways could possibly be found to solve the problem.[11]

The second problem seems more tractable. In connection with his work on counterfactual conditionals, Nicholas Rescher (1964) has developed a method of classifying sentences in modal categories as a basis for choosing maximal consistent subsets. A modal categorization can roughly be described as a sequence of sets of sentences (the sets obeying certain conditions of closedness) where every set includes the preceding set, arranged according to how fundamental the sentences in each set are. A maximal consistent subset is built by adding sentences starting with the most fundamental category and proceeding down the sequence. Depending on the criteria of fundamentality, different categorizations with different properties, are obtained. Hayes suggests as a suitable criterion the theory of causal ordering proposed by Herbert Simon (see Simon & Rescher, 1966).

Given that one could somehow be reconciled with the problem of decidability, we are still very far from a solution to the frame problem. The ideas of subset construction outlined above must be developed into a usable method using specific categorizations. But the problem of elaborating a suitable theory of categories of fundamentality—indeed, a metaphysical problem—is on the whole just a reformulation of the frame problem in a different vocabulary, and Simon's theory of causal ordering gives nothing but hints. Even if we had that theory it is still difficult to believe that the consistency method would be reasonably efficient. It is too explicitly occupied with managing non-changes.

The basic idea of inertness, however, is attractive. It has survived and reappears in several later proposals. One difficulty lies in formulating this

---

[11] But Hayes remains a strict deductivist and he can see no other way out than to drastically constrain the expressive power of the language to make it decidable.

principle in a suitable procedural form; the metaphysical principle of inertness is too vague to guide the design of an efficient procedure.

STRIPS

In STRIPS (Fikes & Nilsson, 1971) there is for the first time a clear separation of synchronic and diachronic reasoning. The synchronic reasoning works deductively, the diachronic reasoning uses GPS-like methods. Precisely through not using deductive methods for diachronic reasoning, the frame problem is claimed to have been overcome. The main principle is that *all that is not explicitly changed by an action remains unchanged*. Although based on the same principle of inertness as the consistency method, the superior computing power of the STRIPS principle is apparent: There is no need to consider *in any way* that which is not explicitly changed.

The following description is limited to the *modeling* mechanism of STRIPS. An action is represented by: (a) a set of preconditions; (b) a delete list; and (c) an add list. An action may be applied in a certain situation if the preconditions are satisfied. The result is that everything in the description that matches the delete list is removed, and the items in the add list are added to form a description of the new situation.

An example: the definition of an operator push(k,m,n) (with semantics: object k is moved from m to n by the robot):

Preconditions:	$ATR(m) \wedge AT(k,m)$
Delete:	$ATR(m)$, $AT(k,m)$
Add:	$ATR(n)$, $AT(k,n)$

where k, m, n, are parameters to be instantiated before applying the operator. (Semantics: $ATR(x)$, the robot is at x; $AT(x,y)$, object x is at y). The definition may be supplemented by synchronic laws, like:

$$\forall u \forall x \forall y \, (AT(u,x) \wedge (x \neq y) \rightarrow \neg AT(u,y))$$

(Semantics: If an object is at one place, it is not at another).

All diachronic knowledge is contained in operator definitions. As we have noted, the use of logic and deductive methods may at first give the impression that STRIPS belongs to the deductivist tradition. There are also additional features that are typically deductivistic, such as a reductionist tendency. But diachronic reasoning is actually GPS-like.

The add and delete lists cannot in general include everything to be changed, since very detailed lists cannot be very general and it should be possible for the effects of an action to vary with the situation. The step taken to compensate for this limitation is to define a set of *primitive* predicates to

Here is an example of a *consequent theorem:*[12]

```
(CONSEQUENT (BLACK ?X)
  (GOAL (RAVEN ?X))
  (OR (GOAL (FRENCH ?X))
    (GOAL (ENGLISH ?X))))
```

This theorem represents that all French and English ravens are black, or rather, *to show that X is black, try to show that X is a raven, and if it succeeds, try to show that it is French, or if that fails, try to show that it is English*[13]—theorems are normally construed as *inference procedures.* The language contains no general mechanism of inference, so the programmer has to provide the system with a theorem for each (elementary) inference that should be possible. This particular theorem about ravens, for example, cannot be used to make any other inference based on the same underlying fact that *all French and English ravens are black.* If we wish that *X is black* should be inferred from *X is a French raven,* we have to construct another theorem, for example:

```
(ANTECEDENT (RAVEN ?X)
  (GOAL (FRENCH ?X))
  (ASSERT (BLACK ?X)))
```

Contrary to the consequent theorem above, which derives implicit information without changing the database, this *antecedent theorem* explicitly adds the derived information to the database. Whenever something of the form (RAVEN ...) is added to the database this theorem will be alerted, and if it succeeds in showing that (FRENCH ...) it will add (BLACK ...) to the database.

Thus, a fact or law, and its intended use, are inseparable in the representation as theorems—PLANNER implies *proceduralism,* a movement within the non-deductivist tradition which advocates the amalgamating of heuristics and epistemology into procedures. Heuristics swallows epistemology. The contrary point of view, *declarativism,* has a more conservative attitude to logic; just as in natural language, the information that *all ravens are black* should be represented in a way neutral to several different types of application. Applying different general mechanisms of inference it is possible to use that declarative information in a variety of ways.

---

[12] The notation is somewhat modified.

[13] The information that the object is French, need not be explicitly in the database. With the GOAL mechanism it suffices if it can be inferred using other consequent theorems.

Nor is there in PLANNER any formal distinction between synchronic reasoning, as in the examples above, and diachronic reasoning, as for example:

(CONSEQUENT (MOVE ?OBJ ?LOC)
  (EXISTS (?X ?Y)
  (GOAL (HOLDS ?OBJ))   ⎫
  (GOAL (ATR ?X))   ⎬ corresponds to preconditions of
  (GOAL (AT ?OBJ ?Y))   ⎭ STRIPS
  (ERASE (ATR ?X))   ⎫
  (ERASE (AT ?OBJ ?Y))   ⎬ corresponds to delete list of STRIPS
  (ASSERT (ATR ?LOC))   ⎫
  (ASSERT (AT ?OBJ ?LOC))))   ⎬ corresponds to add list of STRIPS

An interesting point about PLANNER is that antecedent theorems together with the third type of theorems, *erasing theorems,* provide tools useful in managing parallel effects. The cup-and-saucer example can be handled with the following two pairs of theorems:

(ANTECEDENT (AT ?OBJ ?LOC)   (ERASING (AT ?OBJ ?LOC)
  (EXISTS (?X ?Y)   (EXISTS (?X)
  (GOAL (AT ?X ?Y))   (GOAL (SUPPORTS ?X ?OBJ))
  (GOAL (IMMEDIATELY-BENEATH   (ERASE (SUPPORTS ?X ?OBJ))))
        ?Y ?LOC))
  (ASSERT (SUPPORTS ?X ?OBJ))))

The first pair of theorems administrates the SUPPORTS relation. The following pair administrates the AT relation:[14]

(ANTECEDENT (AT ?OBJ ?LOC)   (ERASING (AT ?OBJ ?LOC)
  (EXISTS (?X ?Y)   (EXISTS (?X ?Y)
  (GOAL (SUPPORTS ?OBJ ?X))   (GOAL (SUPPORTS ?OBJ ?X))
  (GOAL (IMMEDIATELY-BENEATH   (ERASE (AT ?X ?Y))))
        ?LOC ?Y))
  (ASSERT (AT ?X ?Y))))

As soon as an object's place is changed (by erasing (AT object old-place) and asserting (AT object new-place)), the first erasing theorem, responding to the erasure, will try to find out if there is an object that supports the object to be moved—if so, the SUPPORT relation is erased. Similarly, the

---

[14] As it happens, the antecedent theorems are poorly organized: For example, it is inefficient to search for (AT ?X ?Y) before (SUPPORTX ?OBJ ?X).

second erasing theorem finds out if there is some object supported by the object to be moved—if so, its old place is erased. The antecedent theorems will respond to the addition of (AT object new-place)—the first by finding out if the new place is on top of some object, in which case a new SUPPORT relation will be added—the second by finding out if there was an object on top of the moved object, if so, its new place is added (the last theorem invocation is thus directly involved in effecting the desired parallel effect).

Of course, PLANNER is not (and has not been claimed to be) a solution to the frame problem; it is a programming language, and as such, leaves most of the really hard problems to the programmer: making sure that erasures keep pace with additions, preventing theorems from running amok jamming the database in a combinatorial explosion of additions, making sure that theorems are effectively organized and do not lead to fatal contradictions, etc. (See Moore, 1975, for a discussion of the limitations of the procedural deduction used in PLANNER-like systems.) Even the outlined method for managing parallel effects is not without problems —it remains essential to keep down the number of parallel effects or find ways of avoiding handling them explicitly, which mainly is a question of organizing the system's view of the world properly, that is, a metaphysical question. For example, if a robot represents positions of things in a self-centered coordinate system, a simple change of location will have immense parallel effects.

Then, of course, there are the general declarativist and deductivist objections to the proceduralism in PLANNER. Declarative information does not set bounds to the ways it can be exploited, some of which may not be thought of at the time when the information is acquired. In contrast, procedural information demands a completely new representation for each new application. Also, there is no clear connection between different procedures operating with the same underlying declarative information, greatly increasing the risk of inconsistencies and obscuring an overall view. Erik Sandewall (1972b) thinks that the integration of epistemology and heuristics will simply make the construction task for nontrivial problem worlds too big; the separation of modeling and heuristics seems to be a very natural and suitable division into subtasks.

Unless

Erik Sandewall's proposal (1972b) is formulated within a system (Sandewall, 1972a) that in several respects deviates from the original deductivistic paradigm. Predicate logic is not used in the usual straightforward way of letting properties and relations in the problem world be represented by predicates. Instead, there is a limited set of predicates that takes as arguments both objects, properties, and situations. For example, IS(banana, yellow,s) represents the fact that the banana is yellow in situation s.[15] Other examples: EXISTS-IN(banana,yellow) that the banana is yellow in all situations where it exists. A more definitive break with the old paradigm is to allow actions to be part of the description of a situation; for example, INN(push(banana,x,y),s) representing that the banana is pushed from x to y in the situation s. This makes it possible for the system to reason about actions and events. For example, we could have an axiom

INN(push(o,x,y),s) ∧ INN(support(o,o'),s) ⊃ INN(push(o',x,y),s)

Applied to the cup-and-saucer example, the axiom will have the effect that when the saucer is pushed, the cup is simultaneously pushed. Sandewall's approach to the problems of parallel effects is thus to trade the parallel effects for *parallel actions*, the effects of which are deduced in the same way as for any ordinary action.

Sandewall's approach to the frame problem in general is based on the same principle of inertness that figures in Hayes's consistency-based method and in STRIPS. This principle is formulated as an inference rule which says (informally) that: If an object has a certain property in the old situation, and it can not be proved to have lost that property in the new situation, then the object still has the property in the new situation. Formally:

IS(o,p,s)
UNLESS(ENDS(o,p,Succ(s,a)))
──────────────────────────
IS(o,p,Succ(s,a))

where Succ(s,a) is the new situation that results if action a is performed in situation s. We have here not only objects, properties, relations, and actions in a situation, but also *endings* (and there is still more).

The operator UNLESS has the extraordinary property that UNLESS(X) is proved exactly in those cases where X cannot be proved.[16] With this operator we have abandoned the monotonicity of ordinary logic:

If A and B are axiom systems with A⊂ B, then Th(A)⊂ Th(B), where Th(s) = the set of sentences that can be proved from S.

That is, if an axiom system A is extended to a more comprehensive system B, all the old theorems will remain theorems in the new system. If nonmonotonic inferences, like the one with UNLESS above, is introduced, this property is lost. One example: Given an axiom system with A and

---

[15] The notation and syntax are somewhat modified.
[16] There is a similar device in PLANNER: THNOT.

UNLESS(C)B as the only proper axioms, B will be a theorem since we can not prove C:

A, UNLESS(C) → B ⊢ B;

but if the axiom C is added, B is no longer a theorem:

A, UNLESS(C) → B, C, ⊬ B.

Some problems with non-monotonicity will be discussed in the next section.

The representation of an action can be more or less specific in describing the effects of the action; it can be of different degrees of (let us call it) *specificity*. The actions of the blocks–world have a very high degree of specificity—we might even say *total* specificity: Given a description of a situation and an action, the action will never result in a reduced-information content in the new description; it is as detailed as the old one. The total specificity of the blocks–world is a realization of an ideal of total representation, total knowledge of the problem–world, that is part of the early deductivist paradigm.

In less trivial problem—worlds it will be neither possible nor desirable to avoid actions of specificity less than total. Therefore, it seems that Sandewall's proposal is open to the following type of objection: Suppose we have an action *throw a stone at the window* and a window consisting of several small and unbroken panes; and suppose we have arranged that exactly one of the panes will break when the action is performed, but the action has such a low degree of specificity that there is no way of predicting (proving) which particular one it will be. Since we cannot prove that any particular pane ends up being in one piece, we may, using the inference rule above, conclude that all panes remain unbroken in the new situation.

However, the predicate ENDS does not have the semantics that its name suggests. This is not clear from Sandewall (1972b), but Sandewall (1972a) informs us that ENDS(o,p,s) does not imply that —IS(o,p,s). The meaning of ENDS is thus closer to *may end* than to *ends*. It is now a simple matter to let the throwing result in a situation where each windowpane *may have ended* unbroken.

It is clear then, that the predicate ENDS really just serves to mark something as a possible candidate for change; we are left with a local frame problem, once again. More important—we have no guidance for the use of ENDS. What ENDS-effects should an action have? There are few formal restrictions in Sandewall's system, hardly any axioms giving rules for the ENDS predicate.[17] With lavish use of ENDS-effects associated with each

---

[17] There is a small attempt in that direction in Sandewall (1972a) where it is postulated that if ENDS is true of a certain property p of an object, the ENDS is true of every property of the object that is a subproperty of p.

action, a robust and general system could be built, at the cost of a very large local frame problem. On the other hand, with a sufficiently clever organization we could probably make do with quite sparse use of ENDS-effects, thus keeping the local frame problem small. What is this organization like? Well, there's the frame problem again, in a slightly different formulation.

TMS

Truth maintenance systems are systems constructed mainly to aid in revising a knowledge base when conflicts arise, which make them highly interesting in connection with the revision problem. But truth maintenance systems do have some relevance to the frame problem as well, so I will describe the system of Jon Doyle (1978, 1979).[18]

The two datastructures of the system are: *nodes* representing *beliefs* and *justifications* representing *reasons for beliefs*. A node may be *in* or *out*, meaning that the system has, or has not, the corresponding belief. That the system does not have a certain belief does not imply that it believes in its negation. Also, there is in principle nothing to stop the system from simultaneously believing a proposition and its negation; in other words, a node representing p, and a node representing-p, may both be in at the same time.

A justification consists (in the most common case) of a pair of lists: an inlist and an outlist. A node is *in* if and only if it has some justification (there might be several for the same node) the inlist of which contains only nodes that are in, and the outlist of which contains only nodes that are out. Thus, non-monotonic reasoning is a fundamental design characteristic of the system. An *assumption* is a node the justifications of which all have non-empty outlists.

An example will illustrate these concepts:

		Justifications:	
		inlist	outlist
(N1)	The weather will be fine	< (N2)	, (N3) > in
(N2)	Be optimistic about the weather	< (...)	, (...) > in
(N3)	It is going to rain	< (N4,N5)	, ( ) > out
(N4)	It may be assumed that the weather forecast is correct	< (...)	, (...) > in
(N5)	The weather forecast says rain	no justification	out

Starting in this situation, if N5 is given some justification that makes it in, N3 will become in and consequently the assumption N1 out. Of course,

---

[18] The name is rather misleading. *Consistency maintenance* would be better, but even that is quite an exaggeration.

TMS takes no notice of what the nodes happen to stand for; I have added sentences to the nodenames just to give a hint at how the system could be used.

TMS is an attempt to overcome three related problems which all, according to Doyle, have to do with non-monotonicity. They are: (a) the revision problem, (b) the frame problem, and (c) the problem of common-sense reasoning. The contribution of TMS to the solution of these problems is belief-revision: the system can

1. automatically adjust what is to be in and what is to be out when a new justification for a node is added—the addition may cause the node to be in, which in its turn may have the effect that other nodes, the justification of which rests on that node, have to be changed from out to in or vice versa, and so on;

2. when justification for a contradiction is added, the system can automatically perform a belief-revision so as to make the contradiction node out (if possible). A *contradiction* is a special type of node, the justification of which consists of a list of nodes representing beliefs that together constitute a contradiction.

The technique used by TMS in trying to resolve a contradiction is called *dependency-directed backtracking* (Stallman & Sussman, 1971): The system tracks backwards to the fundamental assumptions that are in at the highest possible level and which directly or indirectly give support to the contradiction, chooses one of these assumptions as a *culprit* and makes it out by making one of the nodes in its outlist in (justified by the contradiction). The choice of culprit, or way of making the culprit out, may later prove to be wrong; a new contradiction will then show up and the process is iterated; other ways of making the culprit out, and other culprits, are tried in turn proceeding to assumptions at lower levels until no contradiction shows up (or all possibilities are exhausted and the system has to give up).

Non-monotonic reasoning leads to some logical peculiarities (also discussed in Sandewall (1972b). Consider the following example from Doyle (1979):

(F)	$X + Y = 4$	some support	in
(G)	$X = 1$	$<(J),(\ )>$	in
(H)	$Y = 3$	$<(K),(\ )>$	out

where it is assumed that J is in and K out so that G is in and H out. It is also assumed that F is in for some reason not dependent on G, H, J, or K. If we add to H the justification $<(F,G),(\ )>$, a safe decision as we are doing just ordinary arithmetics, H will become in. If J for some reason becomes out (hence also G) but K becomes in instead (hence also H), we may likewise add to G the justification $<(F,H),(\ )>$ on sound mathematical grounds, and G will again be in. If now K becomes out, so that both J and K are out, we are left with a pair of self-supporting nodes: G is in because H is in, and H is in because G is in! And yet by now X might be 0 and Y be 4.

Doyle (1979) identifies two other types of circularity. There is one type of circularity where at least one of the involved nodes has to be out, a sort of multi-stable arrangement. And there is a paradoxical type of circularity where no combination of in- and out-states is consistent. TMS allows neither of these types of circularities.

No doubt, systems like TMS have an important role to play in the solution of the revision problem. It should be clear from the description of the belief-revision mechanism, however, that the really hard organizational problems are left to the programmer: organizing the information in levels, engineering contradictions, and so on. TMS is not in itself a mechanism for revision of the type called for by the prediction problem, but rather an implementational tool for such revision systems.

Let us return to the frame problem itself. Belief-changes in connection with actions or events are of an essentially non-monotonic nature, Doyle (1979) claims; at one moment the robot believes that the vase is on the table, in the next moment, as a consequence of a move operation, it believes that the vase is on the floor and—*voilà*—the old belief that the vase is on the table has disappeared. We must not forget, however, that there already *is* a solution to the *problem of vanishing beliefs*, which is to introduce situations, so that a belief is always connected to, or restricted to, a situation. Non-monotonicity in the sense of vanishing beliefs *can* in fact be modeled by ordinary monotonic logic.

There seems to be a conflation between certain modes of reasoning and certain technical peculiarities of ordinary logic. It should be clear that monotonicity and non-monotonicity are properties of formal systems, not properties of reasoning, nor of the world. Overlooking this fact results in confusion. It is a trivial fact about non-static problem-worlds, that representations of the world at one moment will have to differ from representations of the world at other moments; provided we agree at all with the possibility of isolating *representations of the world at one moment* from the total representation. (Notice that this does not imply that the representation itself has to change with time.) Where is the non-monotonicity? Only in the eye of the beholder; non-monotonicity is an artifact of logic.

Then what makes many of the proposed non-monotonic methods of reasoning interesting and new is not that they have a non-monotonic appearance when formulated in the language of logic, but other things, such as their use of knowledge about knowledge or lack of knowledge. It is unfortunate that the term *non-monotonic* has come to stand for these important, but poorly understood, modes of reasoning. By this misnomer, questions as disparate as reasoning from lack of knowledge and the problem of vanishing beliefs are brought under a common heading, a heading which can easily lead one to believe that these are all just technical problems of logic.

Some Related Ideas

Although I think we have now covered the main themes in the work on the frame problem, there remain quite a few research ideas and results that seem to have some relation to this problem. Some of the research is performed outside of AI. I will quickly go through a few of the contributions in this category, without going into details.

Non-monotonic logic, Circumscription, and Default reasoning are three different attempts to breathe new life into the deductivist tradition by extending logic to allow for non-monotonic inferences.

Non-monotonic logic (McDermott & Doyle, 1980; McDermott, 1982) is the most general approach. It is an attempt to develop a radically new deductive system permitting non-monotonic inferences of a general type. A complete and rigorous formulation of such a logic does not yet exist; for example, the model theory is incomplete and it is doubtful whether it can be completed (Davis, 1980). These doubts seem to be shared by McDermott himself: ". . . [Non-monotonic logic] is not that well understood, and what is well understood about it is not all that encouraging" (McDermott, 1982b, p. 119).

Circumscription (McCarthy, 1980) and *Default reasoning* (Reiter, 1980) are more specific about the type of non-monotonic inference. Circumscription is based on the idea of *jumping to conclusions:* ". . . the objects that can be shown to have a certain property P by reasoning from certain facts A are all the objects that satisfy P" (McCarthy, 1980, p. 27). Default reasoning is based on the idea of *defaults,* a set of rules to use when information is lacking.

Dynamic logic (Harel, 1979) is a rather conservative extension of ordinary, *static* logic to handle processes conveniently. It is thus explicitly concerned with time and change. The research is mainly motivated by applications to program verification and program synthesis, but applications to *logic of action* have been considered as well. Dynamic logic is solidly founded on the situation concept—despite some notational conveniences and a more elegant treatment compared to the situation calculus, there is nothing really new with respect to the frame problem.

On the whole, there is less to learn from *temporal logic* than might be expected. One reason is that philosophers and logicians working in this field have paid little attention to commonsense time, naive time. Here, I will consider only a contribution by McDermott (1982b), that has no obvious relation to classical works on temporal logic, such as Prior (1967). Again, we find the situation concept at bottom, but the concepts of action and event are less restricted than in the original deductivist paradigm. For example, events are not identified with state changes, and are allowed to take time. The frame problem is addressed somewhat *en passant* with the hope that this temporal logic will make it possible to reason about facts *from the side*, inferring that they are true for whole stretches of time. Although several new concepts are introduced, and although many interesting observations are made (e.g., "when we see a boulder, our eyes are telling our data base about a persistence, not about an instantaneous fact" [McDermott, 1982b, p. 122]),it is at this stage difficult to get an overall picture of McDermott's theory, and in particular to appreciate its relevance to the frame problem.

PART 3: DISCUSSION AND CONCLUSIONS

Metaphysics

Metaphysics is a key concept in my attempt to analyze the frame problem —actually, I think, a concept essential for a proper understanding of a wide range of representational issues in AI. Metaphysics is sometimes thought to be a rather obscure topic, and there are metaphysical issues that I believe are totally irrelevant in this context—materialism vs. idealism is a typical example—so it is perhaps in order that I make myself a bit more clear.

Some examples of metaphysical questions relevant to the frame problem are: What are the fundamental entities? What are the fundamental presuppositions? What basic categories are there? What basic principles? To call these questions metaphysical is to indicate that they are related to empirical evidence only in a very indirect way. It is not important to the arguments and conclusions of this paper whether *metaphysics* is taken in the classical absolute sense (Aristotle, Descartes, Kant) or in the modern relative sense. In the classical sense, *metaphysics* is about the way the world fundamentally is, or the way it is necessarily apprehended. In this sense there can be only one true metaphysics. In the modern sense *metaphysics* concerns fundamental presuppositions, conceptual frameworks in general. Several different, to some degree interchangeable or complementary, metaphysical systems are conceivable. These may differ in efficiency, fruitfulness, or heuristic power, and may be more or less specialized to different aspects of the world.

Whether the metaphysics is believed to reside in the world or in the mind, it will have to be deliberately put into the problem-solving system. Of course, every system will have *some* metaphysics. The point is that it matters which, and that it will not be the right one by chance, or by some force of nature, or by some process in which the designer of the system unwittingly transfers his own metaphysics. All these possibilities are contradicted by experience from the frustrated efforts to solve the frame problem reported in Part 2.

To avoid confusion, let *common sense* refer to the commonsense view of common sense. The metaphysics actually used by human beings in a commonsense world, I will refer to as the *operative* (human) metaphysics. Many of the metaphysical systems that have been advanced by philosophers do not appeal to common sense. (Some do, but they still end up very different from our commonsense view.) On the contrary, the typical metaphysics is very different from common sense.

Why is AI then confined to common sense? Would perhaps a more sophisticated, less naive, metaphysics solve some problems? I think that very few researchers within AI have pondered much over these matters, but one can think of various reasons for sticking to common sense: For example: (a) Our operative metaphysics is the true metaphysics; (b) since it is difficult to construct a suitable metaphysics, let us use the one that is already there, and which we all know (now of course, our operative metaphysics is not as unambiguous and easily accessible as that); and (c) a more powerful argument is the argument from communication—problem-solving systems and human beings will not be able to communicate if they do not have a common way of categorizing the world. If a robot is to be of any significance to a human being, they have to coexist in the same conceptual world. The robot will have tremendous difficulties in picking up a chair if *thing* is not among its fundamental categories; or rather, if it cannot easily decompose *thing* into those fundamental entities. Awkward translation processes will hamper its activities, its observations and reasoning. To understand a command, for example, it will have to unload the command from the user's metaphysical vehicle and then reload the information on its own metaphysical vehicle.

Thus, it appears that, at least as long as we busy ourselves with commonsense problem–worlds, it is not advisable to deviate much from common sense. We must be careful, however, not to make the mistake of assuming that our operative metaphysics is trivial and lies open to inspection for anyone who cares to look at it. Evidence to the contrary comes from philosophy, psychology, linguistics, and—the frustrations of AI. What goes under the name of "common sense" in AI is mostly a curious mixture of Aristotelian and Newtonian mechanics, not strikingly commonsensical, and not to be uncritically accepted as the operative metaphysics.[19] Com-

---

[19] A rather isolated example of a more serious effort within AI to lay bare a part of commonsense physics and metaphysics are the works by Patrick Hayes on *naive physics* (1978a, 1979b), although he does not make what I consider to be the crucial distinction between physics and metaphysics.

paring common sense with science we would expect that the operative metaphysics is much more sophisticated and complex than the metaphysics of science since, contrary to popular belief, the world of common sense is enormously more complex than the world(s) of science. A major reason for the success of science is probably its simplified metaphysics. It may be that the following quote from Popper (1969, p. 137) has some relevance also to AI:

> There is a widespread belief, somewhat remotely due, I think, to the influence of Francis Bacon, that one should study the problems of the theory of knowledge in connection with our knowledge of an orange rather than our knowledge of the cosmos. I dissent from this belief. . .

The irritatingly slow progress in the research on commonsense reasoning *could* be an indication that we are prematurely attacking the really hard problems before we have mastered the more tractable ones.

AI has, on the whole, overlooked the importance of metaphysical deliberations, which has resulted in a proliferation of unpremeditated or ad-hoc metaphysical assumptions; metaphysical questions can be avoided, metaphysical commitments cannot. I think that finding and implementing the adequate metaphysics is a promising approach to the frame problem, as well as an important key to successful modeling in AI in general. Of course, it is far from obvious what an "adequate metaphysics" is, philosophers have searched and quarreled for thousands of years. Rather it is my belief that a better awareness of metaphysical issues, and more conscious efforts to explore and represent adequate metaphysical systems, are important elements of a viable research strategy—a necessary counterbalance to the prevailing tendency of letting work on representational issues be governed by which technical opportunities are seen.

To me, it appears that "experimental ontology" is an apt description of much of what goes on in Knowledge Representation in AI.[20] I don't claim that philosophy has the answers, but I think that any significant progress will hinge on our ability to acquire a philosophical perspective.

The Situation Concept

From the critical examination in Part 2, it appears plausible that the situation concept is an unsuitable foundation for a metaphysics of change. We have found that STRIPS, PLANNER, and TMS, all of which make no explicit use of situations, have in common no need to consider things that do not change. Unchanged facts simply remain. In contrast, every deductivistic system has to process every fact, including those that do not change.

---

[20] This should stir the philosophers, unless they think that philosophy should stick to unsolvable problems.

This should not be confused with the fact that logic is *permissive,* not *imperative* (Minsky, 1974), which is something different. The permissiveness of logic makes it necessary to detach the heuristic component of deductivistic systems from the logic itself, but this does not affect the modeling.

The situation concept goes back to seventeenth-century physics. But in current physics there is nothing left of its former metaphysical status; although it is still sometimes used as a convenient computational device, it is not granted any real significance, being outdated by the theory of relativity and by quantum theory. Neither is there any evidence that the situation concept is part of our operative metaphysics. If one believes (as I do) that the operative metaphysics is at least partially reflected in natural language, linguistics offers a wealth of evidence for contrary hypotheses about our fundamental operative concepts of time and change: Rather than latitudinal, absolute entities, one finds longitudinal, relative entities.[21]

What still might seem to speak in favor of the situation concept is its simplicity. But this is a devious simplicity. What is in a moment? Time derivatives, dispositions, past facts, past possibilities, even future facts and future possibilities? There seems to be no limit to what must be loaded into a single situation when trying to make more accurate and clever problem solvers mastering ever more complex environments. We risk ending up with a concept of a situation that encompasses literally all there is and has been and will be and a little more.

But the most important flaw in the situation concept is that it simply does not seem possible to give definitions useful in commonsense type of worlds, of concepts like *action, event, change,* etc, in terms of the situation concept. This is true even for almost trivial problem worlds. The long record of failures to solve the frame problem bears witness to this.

Explicit, Primitive, and Primary

I will exemplify my view on the role of metaphysics in relation to the frame problem by discussing three pairs of concepts—explicit–implicit, primitive–non-primitive, and primary–secondary—and their relationship.

The terms *explicit* and *implicit* have a clear meaning when applied to formal systems. Axioms are explicit, and everything else that can be inferred from the axioms using the rules of inference is implicit. This is satisfactory from a logical point of view, but those concerned with the algorithmic dimension of formal systems, either performing or engineering inferences, have a need for distinguishing between information *actually* inferred, and information that is *in principle* derivable, but is not at hand, either be-

---

[21] The entirely different situation concept of Barwise and Perry (1981) is one example of an approach to time and change that lies much closer to common sense.

cause it has in fact not been inferred, or it was inferred but the result was subsequently dropped or deleted.

Let us reserve *explicit–implicit* for distinguishing between information that is actually at hand (the axioms as *given*), and information that is not (but can be inferred from information at hand); then we shall take *primitive–non-primitive* to stand for what remains of the original logical explicit–implicit distinction, which is a distinction between independent foundational information (the axioms as a *source*), and dependent superstructural information, derivable from the foundational (primitive) information. Both distinctions are the offspring of the notion of derivability, and clearly, where both distinctions apply, implicit information must be non-primitive, and primitive information must be explicit.[22]

Within the deductivist tradition, committed to formal systems, these distinctions are obviously applicable. Outside of the deductivist tradition we find that in STRIPS the *facts* are formulated using a formal system, and even if we depart from the STRIPS-like systems of the non-deductivist tradition but retain a discernible *database*, the explicit–implicit distinction still applies: Sentences in the database are explicit; sentences inferable from the explicit information using the methods of the system are implicit.[23] A policy for administrating how the contents of a model are distributed into explicit and implicit usually rests on some specific notion of *primitive* information, meaning that also the primitive–non-primitive distinction is applicable.

Whether information is explicit or implicit, primitive or non-primitive, are formal questions, decidable without reference to the modeled world outside the system. A given body of information can be axiomatized in many different ways, if it is at all axiomatizable. There is considerable freedom of choice in deciding what should be explicitly and what should be implicitly represented, what should be taken as primitive and what as non-primitive.

Keeping information implicit may in certain circumstances have the advantage, beside the obvious one of saving space, of facilitating the maneuverability and robustness of the model. As an extreme, consider a *completely explicit* representation (if such a thing is possible): This will be a body of information with a very rich underlying structure, a great number of relations between different parts of the representation. When we

---

[22] Here, I don't take *primitive* to imply that it is impossible to derive primitive information from other primitive information (nor, of course, from non-primitive information). In the end, primitive information is primitive by virtue of being designated as such.

[23] Yet, there remains a certain relativity in applying the distinction. Perhaps it would be better to introduce a concept of *degree of implicitness*, defined, for example, as the number of elementary operations needed to produce the information.

wish to make a change in the model, to reflect a possible change of the represented world, we have to make adjustments in many different parts of the model; the model will be cumbersome to handle, adjustments cannot be done efficiently. There is also a great risk of introducing inconsistencies; the high degree of interdependence between different parts makes it very probable that an adjustment that does not completely cover all relevant parts of the model will result in an inconsistent model.

The other extreme of using a *minimally explicit* representation, a form of representation close to the mathematician's ideal of independent axioms, amounts to an "orthogonalization" of the description in, ideally, completely independent parts; a change of one part can never lead to a conflict with other parts. Thus, to be robust, the model should be approximately orthogonal. However, to ensure a maneuverable model, it is also necessary that the choice of "base vectors" corresponds to the structure of the problem world in such a way that the relevant changes and actions can be easily analyzed into components that correspond to the base vectors spanning the description space.[24] Only when this is the case is the efficiency and reliability of the type of adjustments that actually may occur, guaranteed.

Explicit, implicit, primitive, non-primitive, are all properties that apply to the representation. *Primary* and *secondary*, on the other hand, are properties that relate to the world. Secondary phenomena are in some sense less real; they are *epiphenomena* in principle completely reducible to primary phenomena. Conditions of the world described by secondary information are in principle reducible to conditions described by primary information. This means that given a specific notion of *primary* properties we have a basis for an internal notion of *primitive* information corresponding to dependency relations that can be exploited to represent secondary information implicitly. Which information should be stored explicitly is thus a question that cannot be adequately answered without considering the world and its metaphysics.

Of course, the whole idea of a primary–secondary structure, i.e., reductionism, can be questioned. Is it possible or even desirable? The important thing about implicitness is not that it saves space. Organization and access are the vital points. Space is practically unlimited (or will soon be), time is not. Explicitness is in the end self-defeating: The more we have at hand, the greater trouble we have in quickly locating a particular datum, that is, the less at hand each single datum becomes. Something we might call the *immediately-at-handness* of the model is strictly limited, and we must learn to use it wisely.

---

[24] Here, the vector space metaphor breaks down, since we can not expect that the description-space is anything like linear.

Intrinsic Representation

The explicit situation concept of the deductivists exemplifies an ambition to keep metaphysics, rudimentary as it may be, accessible to the system. This is not a consequence of some deeper considerations about the role of metaphysics—it is just part of a general deductivist aim to keep as much as possible as contents of the model, directly accessible to the system, and in fact, metaphysics is frequently mixed up with physics. What I said about the situation concept seems to imply that we should abandon the kind of physicalistic modeling favored by the deductivists. That is not to say that non-deductivist models are phenomenologically inspired—what may appear as a tendency to subjectivism could also be an effect of trying to implement the system's metaphysics as a capacity rather than as explicit knowledge. Ideally, the metaphysics is built into the system, so that it becomes embodied in the form, or medium, of the representation. The system simply obeys it, without being aware of it. The metaphysics is then *intrinsically* represented. In contrast, the deductivist models are highly *extrinsic:* Logic, the building blocks of the model, has few natural isomorphies with the world. It is much more general; the specific form of the actual world has to be externally imposed on it.

An example (adapted from Palmer, 1978) will help to make the difference between intrinsic and extrinsic representation more clear; note that the example has nothing to do with metaphysics. The represented world consists of three objects of differing lengths. The only things we care to represent are the identities of the objects and the relation *is longer than*. In the first representation there are three objects each representing a particular object of the world. The *is longer than* relation is represented by the relation *is arrow-connected to* that holds between representing objects connected by an arrow. The second representation also uses three objects to represent the objects of the world, but the relation *is longer than* is here represented by relation *is wider than*. The first representation is extrinsic with regard to the *is longer than* relation, the second representation is intrinsic. For example, *is longer than* is a transitive relation, which *is wider than* also is but *is arrow-connected to* is not; in this case the transitivity has to be impressed on it and externally maintained. An elaborate and clarifying discussion of these concepts can be found in Palmer (1978).

The greater generality of the extrinsic representation makes it more resource demanding and more cumbersome to handle. It is also more error prone since it has more possibilities to disagree with the world. The advantages of intrinsic representations are: swift operation, moderate requirements on explicit information, and security—some impossible world–states can simply not be modeled.

It should be emphasized that the motive for making the metaphysics explicit to the designer is more compelling than ever. If, as I claim, the metaphysics has a central role in efficient modeling and should be intrinsically represented, then we are faced with the double task of finding or constructing a suitable metaphysics and implementing it intrinsically.[25] In practice there will be a dialectic interplay between these two tasks. We need to be philosophers and computer scientists alike.

REFERENCES

Barwise, J., & Perry, J. (1981). Situations and attitudes. *Journal of Philosophy, 78,* 668–691.

Bobrow, D.G. (1980). Editor's preface. *Artificial Intelligence, 13,* 1–4.

Davis, M. (1980). The mathematics of non-monotonic reasoning. *Artificial Intelligence, 13,* 73–80.

Doyle, J. (1978). *Truth maintenance systems for problem solving* (AI-TR-419). Cambridge, MA: Massachusetts Institute of Technology Artificial Intelligence Laboratory.

Doyle, J. (1979). A truth maintenance system. *Artificial Intelligence, 12,* 231–272.

Fikes, R.E., & Nilsson, N.J. (1971). STRIPS: A new approach to the application of theorem proving to problem solving. *Artificial Intelligence, 2,* 189–208.

Green, C.C. (1969). Application of theorem proving to problem solving. *Proceedings of the International Joint Conference on Artificial Intelligence* (pp. 219–239), Washington, DC.

Harel, D. (1979). *First-order dynamic logic.* Berlin: Springer-Verlag.

Hayes, P.J. (1971). A logic of actions. In B. Meltzer & D. Michie (Eds.), *Machine Intelligence 6* (pp. 495–520). New York: Wiley.

Hayes, P.J. (1973). The frame problem and related problems in artificial intelligence. In A. Elithorn & D. Jones (Eds.), *Artificial and human thinking* (pp. 41–59). San Francisco: Jossey-Bass.

Hayes, P.J. (1978a). *The naive physics manifesto* (Working Papers No. 34). Geneva, Switzerland: Institut pour les Etudes Semantiques et Cognitives, Universite de Geneve, Fondazione Dalle Molle.

Hayes, P.J. (1978b). *Naive physics I: Ontology for liquids* (Working Papers No. 35). Geneva, Switzerland: Institut pour les Etudes Semantiques et Cognitives, University de Geneve, Fondazione Dalle Molle.

Hewitt, C. (1972). *Description and theoretical analysis (using schemata) of PLANNER: A language for proving theorems and manipulating models in a robot* (Reprinted AI-TR-258). Cambridge, MA: Massachusetts Institute of Technology Artificial Intelligence Laboratory.

McCarthy, J. (1968). Programs with common sense. In M. Minsky (Ed.), *Semantic information processing* (pp. 403–417). Cambridge, MA:

---

[25] I don't argue that the *physics* should be intrinsically represented. There is little hope that the (commonsense) physics of the world in all its variations and aspects can be intrinsically represented (Pylyshyn, 1980). Metaphysics, on the other hand, is a relatively small, unified (and unifying) thing.

McCarthy, J. (1977). Epistemological problems of artificial intelligence. *Proceedings of the 5th International Joint Conference on Artificial Intelligence* (pp. 1038–1044), Cambridge, MA.

McCarthy, J. (1980). Circumscription—a form of non-monotonic reasoning. *Artificial Intelligence, 13,* 27–39.

McCarthy, J., & Hayes, P.J. (1969). Some philosophical problems the standpoint of artificial intelligence. In B. Meltzer & D. Michie (Eds.), *Machine Intelligence 4* (pp. 463–502). Edinburgh, Scotland: Edinburgh University Press.

McDermott, D. (1982a). Non-monotonic logic II: Non-monotonic modal theories. *Journal of the Association for Computing Machinery, 29,* 33–57.

McDermott, D. (1982b). A temporal logic for reasoning about processes and plans. *Cognitive Science 6,* pp. 101–155.

McDermott, D., & Doyle, J. (1980). Non-monotonic logic I. *Artificial Intelligence, 13,* 41–72.

Minsky, M. (1974). *A framework for representing knowledge* (Artificial Intelligence Memo 306). Cambridge, MA: Massachusetts Institute of Technology Artificial Intelligence Laboratory. (Reprinted without appendix in P. Winston, Ed., *The psychology of computer vision,* 1975, New York: McGraw-Hill.)

Moore, R. (1975). *Reasoning from incomplete knowledge in a procedural deduction system* (Artificial Intelligence Technical Report No. 347). Cambridge, MA: Massachusetts Institute of Technology.

Newell, A., Shaw, J.C., & Simon, H.A. (1960). Report of a general problem solving program for a computer. *Proceedings of an International Conference on Information Processing* (pp. 252–264). Paris: UNESCO.

Newell, A., & Simon, H.A. (1972). *Human problem solving.* Englewood Cliffs, NJ: Prentice-Hall.

Palmer, S.E. (1978). Fundamental aspects of cognitive representation. In E. Rosch & B.B. Lloyd (Eds.), *Cognition and categorization.* Hillsdale, NJ: Erlbaum.

Popper, K.R. (1969). *Conjectures and refutation* (3rd ed.). London: Routledge and Kegan Paul.

Pratt, V.R. (1978). *Six lectures on dynamic logic* (MIT/LCS/TM-117). Cambridge, MA: Massachusetts Institute of Technology.

Prior, A. (1967). *Past, present and future.* Oxford: Clarendon.

Pylyshyn, Z.W. (1980). Computation and cognition: Issues in the foundations of cognitive science. *Behavioral and Brain Sciences, 3,* 111–169.

Raphael, B. (1971). The frame problem in problem solving systems. In N.V. Findler & B. Meltzer (Eds.), *Artificial intelligence and heuristic programming* (pp. 159–169). Edinburgh, Scotland: Edinburgh University Press.

Reiter, R. (1980). A logic for default reasoning. *Artificial Intelligence, 13,* 81–132.

Rescher, N. (1964). *Hypothetical reasoning.* Amsterdam, Netherlands: North-Holland.

Robinson, J.A. (1965). A machine-oriented logic based on the resolution principle. *Journal of the Association for Computing Machinery, 12,* 23–41.

Sandewall, E. (1972a). *PCF-2, a first-order calculus for expressing conceptual information.* Uppsala, Sweden: Computer Science Department, Uppsala University.

Sandewall, E. (1972b). An approach to the frame problem and its implementation. In B. Meltzer & D. Michie (Eds.), *Machine Intelligence 7* (pp. 195–204). Edinburgh, Scotland: Edinburgh University Press.

Simon, H.A., & Rescher, N. (1966). Cause and counterfactual. *Philosophy of Science, 33,* 323–340.

Stallman, R.M., & Sussman, G.J. (1977). Forward-reasoning and dependency-directed backtracking in a system for computer-aided circuit analysis. *Artificial Intelligence, 9,* 135–196.

Waldinger, R. (1977). Achieving several goals simultaneously. In E.W. Elcock & D. Michie (Eds.), *Machine Intelligence 8* (pp. 94–136). Edinburgh, Scotland: Edinburgh University Press.

CHAPTER 2

Cognitive Wheels:
The Frame Problem of AI

Daniel Dennett

Tufts University

Once upon a time there was a robot, named R1 by its creators. Its only task was to fend for itself. One day its designers arranged for it to learn that its spare battery, its precious energy supply, was locked in a room with a time bomb set to go off soon. R1 located the room, and the key to the door, and formulated a plan to rescue its battery. There was a wagon in the room, and the battery was on the wagon, and R1 hypothesized that a certain action which it called PULLOUT (WAGON, ROOM) would result in the battery being removed from the room. Straightway it acted, and did succeed in getting the battery out of the room before the bomb went off. Unfortunately, however, the bomb was also on the wagon. R1 *knew* that the bomb was on the wagon in the room, but didn't realize that pulling the wagon would bring the bomb out along with the battery. Poor R1 had missed that obvious implication of its planned act.

Back to the drawing board. "The solution is obvious," said the designers. "Our next robot must be made to recognize not just the intended implications of its acts, but also the implications about their side effects, by deducing these implications from the descriptions it uses in formulating

Reprinted from C. Hookaway (ed.), *Minds, Machines and Evolution* © Cambridge University Press 1984, Cambridge, England.

its plans." They called their next model, the robot-deducer, R1D1. They placed R1D1 in much the same predicament that R1 had succumbed to, and as it too hit upon the idea of PULLOUT (WAGON, ROOM) it began, as designed, to consider the implications of such a course of action. It had just finished deducing that pulling the wagon out of the room would not change the color of the room's walls, and was embarking on a proof of the further implication that pulling the wagon out would cause its wheels to turn more revolutions than there were wheels on the wagon—when the bomb exploded.

Back to the drawing board. "We must teach it the difference between relevant implications and irrelevant implications," said the designers, "and teach it to ignore the irrelevant ones." So they developed a method of tagging implications as either relevant or irrelevant to the project at hand, and installed the method in their next model, the robot-relevant-deducer, or R2D1 for short. When they subjected R2D1 to the test that had so un-equivocally selected its ancestors for extinction, they were surprised to see it sitting, Hamlet-like, outside the room containing the ticking bomb, the native hue of its resolution sicklied o'er with the pale case of thought, as Shakespeare (and more recently Fodor) has aptly put it. "Do something!" they yelled at it. "I am," it retorted. "I'm busily ignoring some thousands of implications I have determined to be irrelevant. Just as soon as I find an irrelevant implication, I put it on the list of those I must ignore, and . . ." the bomb went off.

All these robots suffer from the *frame problem*.[1] If there is ever to be a robot with the fabled perspicacity and real-time adroitness of R2D2, robot-designers must solve the frame problem. It appears at first to be at best an annoying technical embarrassment in robotics, or merely a curious puzzle for the bemusement of people working in Artificial Intelligence (AI). I think, on the contrary, that it is a new, deep epistemological problem—accessible in principle but unnoticed by generations of philosophers—brought to light by the novel methods of AI, and still far from being solved. Many people in AI have come to have a similarly high regard for the seri-ousness of the frame problem. As one researcher has quipped, "We have given up the goal of designing an intelligent robot, and turned to the task

---

[1] The problem is introduced by John McCarthy and Patrick Hayes in their 1969 paper. The task in which the problem arises was first formulated in McCarthy 1960. I am grateful to John McCarthy, Pat Hayes, Bob Moore, Zenon Pylyshyn, John Haugeland and Bo Dahlbom for the many hours they have spent trying to make me understand the frame problem. It is not their fault that so much of their instruction has still not taken.

I have also benefited greatly from reading an unpublished paper, "Modelling Change—the Frame Problem," by Lars-Erik Janlert, Institute of Information Processing, University of Umea, Sweden. It is to be hoped that a subsequent version of that paper will soon find its way into print, since it is an invaluable *vademecum* for any neophyte, in addition to advancing several novel themes.

of designing a gun that will destroy any intelligent robot that anyone else designs!"

I will try here to present an elementary, non-technical, philosophical introduction to the frame problem, and show why it is so interesting. I have no solution to offer, or even any original suggestions for where a solution might lie. It is hard enough, I have discovered, just to say clearly what the frame problem is—and is not. In fact, there is less than perfect agreement in usage within the AI research community. McCarthy and Hayes, who coined the term, use it to refer to a particular, narrowly conceived problem about representation that arises only for certain strategies for dealing with a broader problem about real-time planning systems. Others call this broader problem the frame problem—"the whole pudding," as Hayes has called it (personal correspondence)—and this may not be mere terminological sloppiness. If "solutions" to the narrowly conceived problem have the effect of driving a (deeper) difficulty into some other quarter of the broad problem, we might better reserve the title for this hard-to-corner difficulty. With apologies to McCarthy and Hayes for joining those who would appropriate their term, I am going to attempt an introduction to the whole pudding, calling *it* the frame problem. I will try in due course to describe the narrower version of the problem, "the frame problem proper" if you like, and show something of its relation to the broader problem.

Since the frame problem, whatever it is, is certainly not solved yet (and may be, in its current guises, insoluble), the ideological foes of AI such as Hubert Dreyfus and John Searle are tempted to compose obituaries for the field, citing the frame problem as the cause of death. In *What Computers Can't Do* (Dreyfus, 1972), Dreyfus sought to show that AI was a fundamentally mistaken method for studying the mind, and in fact many of his somewhat impressionistic complaints about AI models and many of his declared insights into their intrinsic limitations can be seen to hover quite systematically in the neighborhood of the frame problem. Dreyfus never explicitly mentions the frame problem,[2] but is it perhaps the smoking pistol he was looking for but didn't *quite* know how to describe? Yes, I

---

[2] Dreyfus mentions McCarthy (1960, pp. 213–214), but the theme of his discussion there is that McCarthy ignores the difference between a *physical state* description and a *situation* description, a theme that might be succinctly summarized: a house is not a home.

Similarly, he mentions *ceteris paribus* assumptions (in the Introduction to the Revised Edition, pp. 56ff.), but only in announcing his allegiance to Wittgenstein's idea that "whenever human behavior is analyzed in terms of rules, these rules must always contain a *ceteris paribus* condition...") But this, even if true, misses the deeper point: the need for something like *ceteris paribus* assumptions confronts Robinson Crusoe just as ineluctably as it confronts any protagonist who finds himself in a situation involving human culture. The point is not, it seems, restricted to *Geisteswissenschaft* (as it is usually conceived); the "intelligent" robot on an (otherwise?) uninhabited but hostile planet faces the frame problem as soon as it commences to plan its days.

think AI can be seen to be holding a smoking pistol, but at least in its "whole pudding" guise it is everybody's problem, not just a problem for AI, which, like the good guy in many a mystery story, should be credited with a discovery, not accused of a crime.

One does not have to hope for a robot-filled future to be worried by the frame problem. It apparently arises from some very widely held and innocuous-*seeming* assumptions about the nature of intelligence, the truth of the most undoctrinaire brand of physicalism, and the conviction that it must be possible to explain how we think. (The dualist evades the frame problem—but only because dualism draws the veil of mystery and obfuscation over all the tough how-questions; as we shall see, the problem arises when one takes seriously the task of answering certain how-questions. Dualists inexcusably excuse themselves from the frame problem.)

One utterly central—if not defining—feature of an intelligent being is that it can "look before it leaps." Better, it can *think* before it leaps. Intelligence is (at least partly) a matter of using well what you know—but for what? For improving the fidelity of your expectations about what is going to happen next, for planning, for considering courses of action, for framing further hypotheses with the aim of increasing the knowledge you will use in the future, so that you can preserve yourself, by letting your hypotheses die in your stead (as Sir Karl Popper once put it). The stupid—as opposed to ignorant—being is the one who lights the match to peer into the fuel tank,[3] who saws off the limb he is sitting on, who locks his keys in his car and then spends the next hour wondering how on earth to get his family out of the car.

But when we think before we leap, *how do we do it?* The answer seems obvious: an intelligent being learns from experience, and then uses what it has learned to guide expectations in the future. Hume explained this in terms of habit of expectation, in effect. *But how do the habits work?* Hume had a hand-waving answer—associationism—to the effect that certain transition paths between ideas grew more likely-to-be-followed as they became well worn, but since it was not *Hume's* job, surely, to explain in more detail the mechanics of these links, problems about how such paths could be put to good use—and not just turned into an impenetrable maze of untraversable alternatives—were not discovered.

Hume, like virtually all other philosophers and "mentalistic" psychologists, was unable to see the frame problem because he operated at what I call a purely semantic level, or a *phenomenological* level. At the phenomenological level, all the items in view are *individuated by their meanings.*

---

[3] The example is from an important discussion of rationality by Christopher Cherniak, in "Rationality and the Structure of Memory," forthcoming in *Synthèse*.

Their meanings are, if you like, "given"—but this just means that the theorist helps himself to all the meanings he wants. In this way the semantic relation between one item and the next is typically plain to see, and one just assumes that the items behave as items with those meanings *ought* to behave. We can bring this out by concocting a Humean account of a bit of learning.

Suppose there are two children, both of whom initially tend to grab cookies from the jar without asking. One child is allowed to do this unmolested but the other is spanked each time she tries. What is the result? The second child learns not to go for the cookies. Why? Because she has had experience of cookie-reaching followed swiftly by spanking. What good does that do? Well, the *idea* of cookie-reaching becomes connected by a habit path to the idea of spanking, which in turn is connected to the idea of pain. . . so *of course* the child refrains. Why? Well, that's just the effect of that idea on that sort of circumstance. But why? Well, what else ought the idea of pain to do on such an occasion? Well, it might cause the child to pirouette on her left foot, or recite poetry or blink or recall her fifth birthday. But given what the idea of pain *means*, any of those effects would be absurd. True; now *how* can ideas be designed so that their effects are what they ought to be, given what they mean? Designing some internal things— an idea, let's call it—so that it behaves *vis-à-vis* its brethren as if it meant *cookie* or *pain* is the only way of endowing that thing with that meaning; it couldn't mean a thing if it didn't have those internal behavioral dispositions.

That is the mechanical question the philosophers left to some dimly imagined future researcher. Such a division of labor might have been all right, but it is turning out that most of the truly difficult and deep puzzles of learning and intelligence get kicked downstairs by this move. It is rather as if philosophers were to proclaim themselves expert explainers of the methods of a stage magician, and then, when we ask them to explain how the magician does the sawing-the-lady-in-half trick, they explain that it is really quite obvious: the magician doesn't really saw her in half; he simply makes it appear that he does. "But how does he do *that*?" we ask. "Not our department," say the philosophers—and some of them add, sonorously: "Explanation has to stop somewhere."[4]

When one operates at the purely phenomenological or semantic level, where does one get one's data, and how does theorizing proceed? The term "phenomenology" has traditionally been associated with an introspective

---

[4] Note that on this unflattering portrayal, the philosophers might still be doing *some* valuable work; think of the wild goose chases one might avert for some investigators who had rashly concluded that the magician really did saw the lady in half and then miraculously reunite her. People have jumped to such silly conclusions, after all; many philosophers have done so, for instance.

method—an *examination* of what is presented or given to consciousness. A person's phenomenology just was by definition the contents of his or her consciousness. Although this has been the ideology all along, it has never been the practice. Locke, for instance, may have thought his "historical, plain method" was a method of unbiased self-observation, but in fact it was largely a matter of disguised aprioristic reasoning about what ideas and impressions *had to be* to do the jobs they "obviously" did.[5] The myth that each of us can observe our mental activities has prolonged the illusion that major progress could be made on the theory of thinking by simply reflecting carefully on our own cases. For some time now we have known better: we have conscious access to only the upper surface, as it were, of the multi-level system of information-processing that occurs in us. Nevertheless, the myth still claims its victims.

So the analogy of the stage magician is particularly apt. One is not likely to make much progress in figuring out *how* the tricks are done by simply sitting attentively in the audience and watching like a hawk. Too much is going on out of sight. Better to face the fact that one must either rummage around backstage or in the wings, hoping to disrupt the performance in telling ways; or, from one's armchair, think aprioristically about how the tricks *must* be done, given whatever is manifest about the constraints. The frame problem is then rather like the unsettling but familiar "discovery" that so far as armchair thought can determine, a certain trick we have just observed is flat impossible.

Here is an example of the trick. Making a midnight snack. How is it that I can get myself a midnight snack? What could be simpler? I suspect there is some leftover sliced turkey and mayonnaise in the fridge, and bread in the breadbox—and a bottle of beer in the fridge as well. I realize I can put these elements together, so I concoct a childishly simple plan: I'll just go and check out the fridge, get out the requisite materials, and make myself a sandwich, to be washed down with a beer. I'll need a knife, a plate, and a glass for the beer. I forthwith put the plan into action and it works! Big deal.

Now of course I couldn't do this without knowing a good deal—about bread, spreading mayonnaise, opening the fridge, the friction and inertia that will keep the turkey between the bread slices and the bread on the plate as I carry the plate over to the table beside my easy chair. I also need to know about how to get the beer out of the bottle and into the glass.[6] Thanks to my previous accumulation of experience in the world, fortunately, I am equipped with all this worldly knowledge. Of course some of the

---

[5] See Dennett (1982a), a commentary on Goodman (1982).

[6] This knowledge of physics is not what one learns in school, but in one's crib. See Hayes (1978, 1979).

knowledge I need *might* be innate. For instance, one trivial thing I have to know is that when the beer gets into the glass it is no longer in the bottle, and that if I'm holding the mayonnaise jar in my left hand I cannot also be spreading the mayonnaise with the knive in my left hand. Perhaps these are straightforward implications—instantiations—of some more funda-mental things that I was in effect *born knowing* such as, perhaps, the fact that if something is in one location it isn't also in another, different loca-tion; or the fact that two things can't be in the same place at the same time; or the fact that situations change as the result of actions. It is hard to imag-ine just how one could learn these facts from experience.

Such utterly banal facts escape our notice as we act and plan, and it is not surprising that philosophers, thinking phenomenologically *but intro-spectively*, should have overlooked them. But if one turns one's back on in-trospection, and just thinks "hetero-phenomenologically"[7] about the purely informational demands of the task—what *must* be known by any entity that can perform this task—these banal bits of knowledge rise to our atten-tion. We can easily satisfy ourselves that no agent that did not *in some sense* have the benefit of the information (that beer in the bottle is not in the glass, etc.) could perform such a simple task. It is one of the chief meth-odological beauties of AI that it makes one be a phenomenologist in this improved way. As a hetero-phenomenologist, one reasons about what the agents must "know" or figure out *unconsciously or consciously* in order to perform in various ways.

The reason AI forces the banal information to the surface is that the tasks set by AI start at zero: the computer to be programmed to simulate the agent (or the brain of the robot, if we are actually going to operate in the real non-simulated world), initially knows nothing at all "about the world." The computer is the fabled *tabula rasa* on which every required item must somehow be impressed, either by the programmer at the outset or via subsequent "learning" by the system.

We can all agree, today, that there could be no learning at all by an entity that faced the world at birth as a *tabula rasa*, but the dividing line be-tween what is innate and what develops maturationally and what is actu-ally learned is of less theoretical importance than one might have thought. While some information has to be innate, there is hardly any particular item that must be: an appreciation of *modus ponens*, perhaps, and the law of the excluded middle, and some sense of causality. And while some things we know must be learned—e.g., that Thanksgiving falls on a Thursday, or that refrigerators keep food fresh—many other "very empirical" things could in principle be innately known—e.g., that smiles mean happiness,

---

[7] For elaborations of hetero-phenomenology, see Dennett (1978, chapter 10, "Two Ap-proaches to Mental Images," and Dennett (1982b). See also Dennett (1982c).

or that unsuspended, unsupported things fall. (There is some evidence, in fact, that there is an innate bias in favor of perceiving things to fall with gravitational acceleration).[8]

Taking advantage of this advance in theoretical understanding (if that is what it is), people in AI can frankly ignore the problem of learning (it seems) and take the shortcut of *installing* all that an agent has to "know" to solve a problem. After all, if God made Adam as an adult who could presumably solve the midnight snack problem *ab initio*, AI agent-creators can *in principle* make an "adult" agent who is equipped with worldly knowledge *as if* it had laboriously learned all the things it needs to know. This may of course be a dangerous shortcut.

The installation problem is then the problem of installing in one way or another all the information needed by an agent to plan in a changing world. It is a difficult problem because the information must be installed in a usable format. The problem can be broken down initially into the semantic problem and the syntactic problem. The semantic problem— called by Allen Newell the problem at the "knowledge level" (Newell, 1982)—is the problem of just what information (on what topics, to what effect) must be installed. The syntactic problem is what system, format, structure, or mechanism to use to put that information in.[9]

The division is clearly seen in the example of the midnight snack problem. I *listed* a few of the very many humdrum facts one needs to know to solve the snack problem, but I didn't mean to suggest that those facts are stored in me—or in any agent—piecemeal, in the form of a long list of sentences explicitly declaring each of these facts for the benefit of the agent. That is of course one possibility, officially: it is a preposterously extreme version of the "language of thought" theory of mental representation, with each distinguishable "proposition" separately inscribed in the

---

[8] Gunnar Johannsen has shown that animated films of "falling" objects in which the moving spots drop with the normal acceleration of gravity are unmistakeably distinguished by the casual observer from "artifical" motions. I do not know whether infants have been tested to see if they respond selectively to such displays.

[9] McCarthy and Hayes (1969) draw a different distinction between the "epistemological" and the "heuristic." The difference is that they include the question "In what kind of internal notation is the system's knowledge to be expressed?" in the epistemological problem (see p. 466), dividing off *that* syntactic (and hence somewhat mechanical) question from the procedural questions of the design of "the mechanism that on the basis of the information solves the problem and decides what to do."

One of the prime grounds for controversy about just which problem the frame problem is springs from this attempted division of the issue. For the answer to the syntactical aspects of the epistemological question makes a large difference to the nature of the heuristic problem. After all, if the syntax of the expression of the system's knowledge is sufficiently perverse, then in spite of the *accuracy* of the representation of that knowledge, the heuristic problem will be impossible. And some have suggested that the heuristic problem would virtually disappear if the world knowledge were felicitously couched in the first place.

system. No one subscribes to such a view; even an encyclopedia achieves important economies of explicit expression via its organization, and a walking encyclopedia—not a bad caricature of the envisaged AI agent—must use different systemic principles to achieve efficient representation and access. We know trillions of things; we know that mayonnaise doesn't dissolve knives on contact, that a slice of bread is smaller than Mount Everest, that opening the refrigerator doesn't cause a nuclear holocaust in the kitchen.

There must be in use—and in any intelligent agent—some highly efficient, partly generative or productive system of representing—storing for use—all the information needed. Somehow, then, we must store many "facts" at once—where facts are presumed to line up more or less one-to-one with non-synonymous declarative sentences. Moreover, we cannot realistically hope for what one might call a Spinozistic solution—a *small* set of axioms and definitions from which all the rest of our knowledge is deducible on demand—since it is clear that there simply are no entailment relations between vast numbers of these facts. (When we rely, as we must, on experience to tell us how the world is, experience tells us things that do not at all follow from what we have heretofore known.)

The demand for an efficient system of information storage is in part a space limitation, since our brains are not all that large, but more importantly it is a time limitation, for stored information that is not reliably accessible for use in the short real-time spans typically available to agents in the world is of no use at all. A creature that can solve any problem given enough time—say a million years—is not in fact intelligent at all. We live in a time-pressured world and must be able to think quickly before we leap. (One doesn't have to view this as an *a priori* condition on intelligence. One can simply note that we do in fact think quickly, so there is an empirical question about how we manage to do it.)

The task facing the AI researcher appears to be designing a system that can plan by using well-selected elements from its store of knowledge about the world it operates in. "Introspection" on how *we* plan yields the following description of a process: one envisages a certain situation (often very sketchily); one then imagines performing a certain act in that situation; one then "sees" what the likely outcome of that envisaged act in that situation would be, and evaluates it. What happens backstage, as it were, to permit this "seeing" (and render it as reliable as it is) is utterly inaccessible to introspection.

On relatively rare occasions we all experience such bouts of thought, unfolding in consciousness at the deliberate speed of pondering. These are occasions in which we are faced with some novel and relatively difficult problem, such as: How can I get the piano upstairs? or Is there any way to electrify the chandelier without cutting through the plaster ceiling? It would be quite odd to find that one had to think *that* way (consciously and slowly) in order to solve the midnight snack problem. But the suggestion is that even the trivial problems of planning and bodily guidance that are beneath our notice (though in some sense we "face" them) are solved by similar processes. Why? I don't *observe* myself planning in such situations. This fact suffices to convince the traditional, introspective phenomenologist that no such planning is going on.[10] The hetero-phenomenologist, on the other hand, reasons that *one way or another* information about the objects in the situation, and about the intended effects and side effects of the candidate actions, *must* be used (considered, attended to, applied, appreciated). Why? Because otherwise the "smart" behavior would be sheer luck or magic. (Do we have any model for how such unconscious information-appreciation might be accomplished? The only model we have *so far* is *conscious*, deliberate information-appreciation. Perhaps, AI suggests, this is a good model. If it isn't, we are all utterly in the dark for the time being.)

We assure ourselves of the intelligence of an agent by considering counterfactuals: if I had been told that the turkey was poisoned, or the beer explosive, or the plate dirty, or the knife too fragile to spread mayonnaise, would I have acted as I did? If I were a stupid "automaton"—or like the *Sphex* wasp who "mindlessly" repeats her stereotyped burrow-checking routine till she drops[11]—I might infelicitously "go through the motions" of making a midnight snack oblivious to the recalcitrant features of the environment.[12] But in fact, my midnight-snack-making behavior is multifar-

---

[10] Such observations also convinced Gilbert Ryle, who was, in an important sense, an introspective phenomenologist (and not a "behaviorist"). See Ryle (1949).

One can readily imagine Ryle's attack, on AI: "And *how many* inferences do I perform in the course of preparing my sandwich? Why syllogisms convince me that the beer will stay in the glass?" For a further discussion of Ryle's skeptical arguments and their relation to cognitive science, see my "Styles of Mental Representations" (Dennett, 1983).

[11] "When the time comes for egg laying the wasp *Sphex* builds a burrow for the purpose and seeks out a cricket which she stings in such a way as to paralyze but not kill it. She drags the cricket into her burrow, lays her eggs alongside, closes the burrow, then flies away, never to return. In due course, the eggs hatch and the wasp grubs feed off the paralyzed cricket, which has not decayed, having been kept in the wasp equivalent of deep freeze. To the human mind, such an elaborately organized and seemingly purposeful routine conveys a convincing flavor of logic and thoughtfulness—until more details are examined. For example, the wasp's routine is to bring the paralyzed cricket to the burrow, leave it on the threshold, go inside to see that all is well, emerge, and then drag the cricket in. If, while the wasp is inside making her preliminary inspection the cricket is moved a few inches away, the wasp, on emerging from the burrow, will bring the cricket back to the threshold, but not inside, and will then repeat the preparatory procedure of entering the borrow to see that everything is all right. If again the cricket is removed a few inches while the wasp is inside, once again the wasp will move the cricket up to the threshold and re-enter the burrow for a final check. The wasp never thinks of pulling the cricket straight in. One one occasion, this procedure was repeated forty times, always with the same results" (Dean Wooldridge, 1963).

This vivid example of a familiar phenomenon among insects is discussed by me in *Brainstorms*, and in Douglas Hofstadter (1982).

[12] See Dennett (1982c, pp. 58–59) on "Robot Theater."

iously sensitive to current and background information about the situation. The only way it could be so sensitive—runs the tacit hetero-phenomenological reasoning—is for it to examine, or test for, the information in question. This information manipulation may be unconscious and swift, and it need not (it *better* not) consist of hundreds or thousands of *seriatim* testing procedures, but it must occur somehow, and its benefits must appear in time to help me as I commit myself to action.

I may of course have a midnight snack routine, developed over the years, in which case I can partly rely on it to pilot my actions. Such a complicated "habit" would have to be under the control of a mechanism of some complexity, since even a rigid sequence of steps would involve periodic testing to ensure that subgoals had been satisfied. And even if I am an infrequent snacker, I no doubt have routines for mayonnaise-spreading, sandwich-making, and getting-something-out-of-the-fridge, from which I could compose my somewhat novel activity. Would such ensembles of routines, nicely integrated, suffice to solve the frame problem for me, at least in my more "mindless" endeavors? That is an open question to which I will return below.

It is important in any case to acknowledge at the outset, and remind oneself frequently, that even very intelligent people do make mistakes; we are not only not infallible planners; we are quite prone to overlooking large and retrospectively obvious flaws in our plans. This foible manifests itself in the familiar case of "force of habit" errors (in which our stereotypical routines reveal themselves to be surprisingly insensitive to some portentous environmental changes while surprisingly sensitive to others). The same weakness also appears on occasion in cases where we have consciously deliberated with some care. How often have you embarked on a project of the piano-moving variety—in which you've thought through or even "walked through" the whole operation in advance—only to discover that you must backtrack or abandon the project when some perfectly foreseeable but unforeseen obstacle or unintended side effect loomed? If we smart folk seldom actually paint ourselves into corners, it may be not because we plan ahead so well as that we supplement our sloppy planning powers with a combination of recollected lore (about fools who paint themselves into corners, for instance) and frequent progress checks as we proceed. Even so, we must know enough to call up the right lore at the right time, and to recognize impending problems as such.

To summarize: we have been led by fairly obvious and compelling considerations to the conclusion that an intelligent agent must engage in swift information-sensitive "planning" which has the effect of producing reliable but not foolproof expectations of the effects of its actions. That these expectations are normally in force in intelligent creatures is testified to by the startled reaction they exhibit when their expectations are thwarted.

This suggests a graphic way of characterizing the minimal goal that can spawn the frame problem: we want a midnight-snack-making robot to be "surprised" by the trick plate, the unspreadable concrete mayonnaise, the fact that we've glued the beer glass to the shelf. To be surprised you have to have expected something else, and in order to have expected the right something else, you have to have *and use* a lot of information about the things in the world.[13]

The central role of expectation has led some to conclude that the frame problem is not a new problem at all, and has nothing particularly to do with planning actions. It is, they think, simply the problem of having good expectations about any future events, whether they are one's own actions, the actions of another agent, or the mere happenings of nature. That is the problem of induction—noted by Hume and intensified by Goodman (1965), but still not solved to anyone's satisfaction. We know today that the problem of induction is a nasty one indeed. Theories of subjective probability and belief fixation have not stabilized in reflective equilibrium, so it is fair to say that no one has a good, principled answer to the general question: given that I believe all *this* (have all this evidence), what *ought* I to believe as well (about the future, or about unexamined parts of the world)?

The reduction of one unsolved problem to another is some sort of progress, unsatisfying though it may be, but it is not an option in this case. The frame problem is not the problem of induction in disguise. For suppose the problem of induction were solved. Suppose—perhaps miraculously— that our agent has solved all its induction problems or had them solved by fiat; it believes, then, all the right generalizations from its evidence, and associates with all of them the appropriate probabilities and conditional probabilities. This agent, *ex hypothesi*, believes just what it ought to believe about all empirical matters in its ken, including the probabilities of future events. It might still have a bad case of the frame problem, for that problem concerns how to represent (so it can be *used*) all that hard-won empirical information—a problem that arises independently of the truth

---

[13] Hubert Dreyfus has pointed out that *not expecting x* does not imply *expecting y* (where $x \neq y$), so one can be startled by something one didn't expect without its having to be the case that one (unconsciously) expected something else. But this sense of *not expecting* will not suffice to explain startle. What are the odds against your seeing an Alfa Romeo, a Buick, a Chevrolet, and a Dodge parked in alphabetical order some time or other within the next five hours? Very high, no doubt, all things considered, so I would not expect you to expect this; I also would not expect you to be startled by seeing this unexpected sight—except in the sort of special case where you had reason to expect something else at that time and place.

Startle reactions are powerful indicators of cognitive state—a fact long known by the police (and writers of detective novels). *Only* someone who expected the refrigerator to contain Smith's corpse (say) would be *startled* (as opposed to mildly interested) to find it to contain the rather unlikely trio: a bottle of vintage Chablis, a can of cat food, and a dishrag.

value, probability, warranted assertability, or subjective certainty of any of it. Even if you have excellent *knowledge* (and not mere belief) about the changing world, how can this knowledge be represented so that it can be efficaciously brought to bear?

Recall poor R1D1, and suppose for the sake of argument that it had perfect empirical knowledge of the probabilities of all the effects of all its actions that would be detectable by it. Thus it believes that with probability 7864, executing PULLOUT (WAGON, ROOM) will cause the wagon wheels to make an audible noise; and with probability 5, the door to the room will open in rather than out; and with probability 999996, there will be no live elephants in the room, and with probability 997 the bomb will remain on the wagon when it is moved. How is R1D1 to find this last, relevant needle in its haystack of empirical knowledge? A walking encyclopedia will walk over a cliff, for all its knowledge of cliffs and the effects of gravity, unless it is designed in such a fashion that it can find the right bits of knowledge at the right times, so it can plan its engagements with the real world.

The earliest work on planning systems in AI took a deductive approach. Inspired by the development of Robinson's methods of resolution theorem proving, designers hoped to represent all the system's "world knowledge" explicitly as axioms, and use ordinary logic—the predicate calculus—to deduce the effects of actions. Envisaging a certain situation S was modeled by having the system entertain a set of axioms describing the situation. Added to this were background axioms (the so-called "frame axioms" that give the frame problem its name) which describe general conditions and the general effects of every action type defined for the system. To this set of axioms the system would apply an action—by postulating the occurrence of some action A in situation S—and then deduce the effect of A in S, producing a description of the outcome situation S'). While all this logical deduction looks like nothing at all in our conscious experience, research on the deductive approach could proceed on either or both of two enabling assumptions: the methodological assumption that psychological realism was a gratuitous bonus, not a goal, of "pure" AI, or the substantive (if still vague) assumption that the deductive processes described would somehow model the backstage processes beyond conscious access. In other words, either we don't do our thinking deductively in the predicate calculus but a robot might; or we do (unconsciously) think deductively in the predicate calculus. Quite aside from doubts about its psychological realism, however, the deductive approach has not been made to work—the proof of the pudding for any robot—except for deliberately trivialized cases.

Consider some typical frame axioms associated with the action type: *move x onto y.*

(1) If $z \neq x$ and I move x onto y, then if z was on w before, then z is on w after.

(2) If x is blue before, and I move x onto y, then x is blue after.

Note that (2), about being blue, is just one example of the many boring "no-change" axioms we have to associate with this action type. Worse still, note that a cousin of (2), also about being blue, would have to be associated with every other action-type—with *pick up x* and with *give x to y*, for instance. One cannot save this mindless repetition by postulating once and for all something like

(3) If anything is blue, it stays blue,

for that is false, and in particular we will want to leave room for the introduction of such action types as *paint x red*. Since virtually any aspect of a situation can change under some circumstance, this method requires introducing for each aspect (each predication in the description of S) an axiom to handle whether that aspect changes for each action type.

This representational profligacy quickly gets out of hand, but for some "toy" problems in AI, the frame problem can be overpowered to some extent by a mixture of the toyness of the environment and brute force. The early version of SHAKEY, the robot at S.R.I., operated in such a simplified and sterile world, with so few aspects it could worry about that it could get away with an exhaustive consideration of frame axioms.[14]

Attempts to circumvent this explosion of axioms began with the proposal that the system operate on the tacit assumption that nothing changes in a situation but what is explicitly asserted to change in the definition of the applied action (Fikes & Nilsson, 1971). The problem here is that, as Garrett Hardin once noted, you can't do just one thing. This was R1's problem, when it failed to notice that it would pull the bomb out with the wagon. In the explicit representation (a few pages back) of my midnight snack solution, I mentioned carrying the plate over to the table. On this proposal, my model of S' would leave the turkey back in the kitchen, for I didn't explicitly say the turkey would come along with the plate. One can of course patch up the definition of "bring" or "plate" to handle just this problem, but only at the cost of creating others. (Will a few more patches tame the problem? At what point should one abandon patches and seek an altogether new approach? Such are the methodological uncertainties regularly encountered in this field, and of course no one can responsibly claim in advance to have a good rule for dealing with them. Premature counsels of

---

[14] This early feature of SHAKEY was drawn to my attention by Pat Hayes. See also Dreyfus (1972, p. 26). SHAKEY is put to quite different use in Dennett (1982b).

despair or calls for revolution are as clearly to be shunned as the dogged pursuit of hopeless avenues; small wonder the field is contentious.)

While one cannot get away with the tactic of supposing that one can do just one thing, it remains true that very little of what could (logically) happen in any situation does happen. Is there some way of fallibly marking the likely area of important side effects, and assuming the rest of the situation to stay unchanged? Here is where relevance tests seem like a good idea, and they may well be, but not within the deductive approach. As Minsky notes:

> Even if we formulate relevancy restrictions, logistic systems have a problem using them. In any logistic system, all the axioms are necessarily "permissive" —they all help to permit new inferences to be drawn. Each added axiom means more theorems; none can disappear. There simply is no direct way to add information to tell such a system about kinds of conclusions that should *not* be drawn! . . . If we try to change this by adding axioms about relevancy, we still produce all the unwanted theorems, plus annoying statements about their irrelevancy. (Minsky, 1981, p. 125)

What is needed is a system that genuinely *ignores* most of what it knows, and operates with a well-chosen portion of its knowledge at any moment. Well-chosen, but not chosen by exhaustive consideration. How, though, can you give a system *rules* for ignoring—or better, since explicit rule-following is not the problem, how can you design a system that reliably ignores what it ought to ignore under a wide variety of different circumstances in a complex action environment?

John McCarthy calls this the qualification problem, and vividly illustrates it via the famous puzzle of the missionaries and the cannibals.

> Three missionaries and three cannibals come to a river. A rowboat that seats two is available. If the cannibals ever outnumber the missionaries on either bank of the river, the missionaries will be eaten. How shall they cross the river?
>
> Obviously the puzzler is expected to devise a strategy of rowing the boat back and forth that gets them all across and avoids disaster . . .
>
> Imagine giving someone the problem, and after he puzzles for awhile, he suggests going upstream half a mile and crossing on a bridge. "What bridge?" you say. "No bridge is mentioned in the statement of the problem." And this dunce replies, "Well, they don't say there isn't a bridge." You look at the English and even at the translation of the English into first order logic, and you must admit that "they don't say" there is no bridge. So you modify the problem to exclude bridges and pose it again, and the dunce proposes a helicopter, and after you exclude that, he proposes a winged horse or that the others hang onto the outside of the boat while two row.

You now see that while a dunce, he is an inventive dunce. Despairing of getting him to accept the problem in the proper puzzler's spirit, you tell him the solution. To your further annoyance, he attacks your solution on the grounds that the boat might have a leak or lack oars. After you rectify that omission from the statement of the problem, he suggests that a sea monster may swim up the river and may swallow the boat. Again you are frustrated, and you look for a mode of reasoning that will settle his hash once and for all. (McCarthy, 1980, pp. 29–30)

What a normal, intelligent human being does in such a situation is to engage in some form of *non-monotonic inference.* In a classical, monotonic logical system, *adding* premises never *diminishes* what can be proved from the premises. As Minsky noted, the axioms are essentially permissive, and once a theorem is permitted, adding more axioms will never invalidate the proofs of earlier theorems. But when we think about a puzzle or a real life problem, we can achieve a solution (and even prove that it is a solution, or even the only solution to *that* problem), and then discover our solution invalidated by the addition of a new element to the posing of the problem; e.g., "I forgot to tell you—there are no oars" or "By the way, there's a perfectly good bridge upstream."

What such late additions show us is that, contrary to our assumption, other things weren't equal. We had been reasoning with the aid of a *ceteris paribus* assumption, and now our reasoning has just been jeopardized by the discovery that something "abnormal" is the case. (Note, by the way, that the abnormality in question is a much sublter notion than anything anyone has yet squeezed out of probability theory. As McCarthy notes, "The whole situation involving cannibals with the postulated properties cannot be regarded as having a probability, so it is hard to take seriously the conditional probability of a bridge given the hypothesis."

The beauty of a *ceteris paribus* clause in a bit of reasoning is that one does not have to say exactly what it means. "What do you mean, other things being equal?" Exactly which arrangements of which other things count as being equal?" If one had to answer such a question, invoking the *ceteris paribus* clause would be pointless, for it is precisely in order to evade that task that one uses it. If one could answer that question, one wouldn't need to invoke the clause in the first place. One way of viewing the frame problem, then, is as the attempt to get a computer to avail itself of this distinctively human style of mental operation. There are several quite different approaches to non-monotonic inference being pursued in AI today. They have in common only the goal of capturing the human talent for *ignoring* what should be ignored, while staying alert to relevant recalcitrance when it occurs.

One family of approaches, typified by the work of Marvin Minsky and Roger Schank (Minsky, 1981; Schank & Abelson, 1977), gets its ignoring-power from the attention-focussing power of stereotypes. The inspiring insight here is the idea that all of life's experiences, for all their variety, boil down to variations on a manageable number of stereotypic themes, paradigmatic scenarios—"frames" in Minsky's terms, "scripts" in Schank's.

An artificial agent with a well-stocked compendium of frames or scripts, appropriately linked to each other and to the impingements of the world via its perceptual organs, would face the world with an elaborate system of what might be called habits of attention and benign tendencies to leap to particular sorts of conclusions in particular sorts of circumstances. It would "automatically" pay attention to certain features in certain environments and assume that certain unexamined normal features of those environments were present. Concomitantly, it would be differentially alert to relevant divergences from the stereotypes it would always begin by "expecting."

Simulations of fragments of such an agent's encounters with its world reveal that in many situations it behaves quite felicitously and apparently naturally, and it is hard to say, of course, what the limits of this approach are. But there are strong grounds for skepticism. Most obviously, while such systems perform creditably when the world co-operates with their stereotypes, and even with *anticipated* variations on them, when their worlds turn perverse, such systems typically cannot recover gracefully from the misanalyses they are led into. In fact, their behavior *in extremis* looks for all the world like the preposterously counterproductive activities of insects betrayed by their rigid tropisms and other genetically hardwired behavioral routines.

When these embarrassing misadventures occur, the system designer can improve the design by adding provisions to deal with the particular cases. It is important to note that in these cases, the system does not redesign itself (or learn) but rather must wait for an external designer to select an improved design. This process of redesign recapitulates the process of natural selection in some regards; it favors minimal, piecemeal, *ad hoc* redesign which is tantamount to a wager on the likelihood of patterns in future events. So in some regards it is faithful to biological themes.[15] Nevertheless, until such a system is given a considerable capacity to learn from its errors without designer intervention, it will continue to respond in insectlike ways, and such behavior is profoundly unrealistic as a model of human reactivity to daily life. Thus shortcuts and cheap methods provided by a reliance on stereotypes are evident enough in human ways of thought,

---

[15] In one important regard, however, it is dramatically unlike the process of natural selection, since the trial, error and selection of the process is far from blind. But a case can be made that the impatient researcher does nothing more than telescope time by such foresighted interventions in the redesign process.

but it is also evident that we have a deeper understanding to fall back on when our shortcuts don't avail, and building some measure of this deeper understanding into a system appears to be a necessary condition of getting it to learn swiftly and gracefully.

In effect, the script or frame approach is an attempt to *pre-solve* the frame problems the particular agent is likely to encounter. While insects do seem saddled with such control systems, people, even when they do appear to be relying on stereotypes, have back-up systems of thought that can deal more powerfully with problems that arise. Moreover, when people do avail themselves of stereotypes, they are at least relying on stereotypes of their own devising, and to date no one has been able to present any workable ideas about how a person's frame-making or script-writing machinery might be guided by its previous experience.

Several different sophisticated attempts to provide the representational framework for this deeper understanding have emerged from the deductive tradition in recent years. Drew McDermott and Jon Doyle have developed a "non-monotonic logic" (1980), Ray Reiter has a "logic for default reasoning" (1980), and John McCarthy has developed a system of "circumscription," a formalized "rule of conjecture that can be used by a person or program for 'jumping to conclusions'" (1980). None of these is, or is claimed to be, a complete solution to the problem of *ceteris paribus* reasoning, but they might be components of such a solution. More recently, McDermott has offered a "temporal logic for reasoning about processes and plans" (McDermott, 1982). I will not attempt to assay the formal strengths and weaknesses of these approaches. Instead I will concentrate on another worry. From one point of view, non-monotonic or default logic, circumscription, and temporal logic all appear to be radical improvements to the mindless and clanking deductive approach, but from a slightly different perspective they appear to be more of the same, and at least as unrealistic as frameworks for psychological models.

They appear in the former guise to be a step towards greater psychological realism, for they take seriously, and attempt to represent, the phenomenologically salient phenomenon of common sense *ceteris paribus* "jumping to conclusions" reasoning. But do they really succeed in offering any plausible suggestions about how the backstage implementation of that conscious thinking is accomplished *in people?* Even if on some glorious future day a robot with debugged circumscription methods maneuvered well in a non-toy environment, would there be much likelihood that its constituent processes, *described at levels below the phenomeno-logical,* would bear informative relations to the unknown lower-level backstage processes in human beings? To bring out better what my worry is, I want to introduce the concept of a *cognitive wheel.*

We can understand what a cognitive wheel might be by reminding ourselves first about ordinary wheels. Wheels are wonderful, elegant triumphs of technology. The traditional veneration of the mythic inventor of the wheel is entirely justified. But if wheels are so wonderful, why are there no animals with wheels? Why are no wheels to be found (functioning as wheels) in nature? First, the presumption of that question must be qualified. A few years ago the astonishing discovery was made of several microscopic beasties (some bacteria and some unicellular eukaryotes) that have wheels of sorts. Their propulsive tails, long thought to be flexible flagella, turn out to be more or less rigid corkscrews, which rotate continuously, propelled by microscopic motors of sorts, complete with main bearings.[16] Better known, if less interesting for obvious reasons, are the tumbleweeds. So it is not quite true that there are no wheels (or wheeliform designs) in nature.

Still, macroscopic wheels—reptilian or mammalian or avian wheels— are not to be found. Why not? They would seem to be wonderful retractable landing gear for some birds, for instance. Once the question is posed, plausible reasons rush in to explain their absence. Most important, probably, are the considerations about the topological properties of the axle/ bearing boundary that make the transmission of material or energy across it particularly difficult. How could the life-support traffic arteries of a living system maintain integrity across this boundary? But once that problem is posed, solutions suggest themselves; suppose the living wheel grows to mature form in a non-rotating, non-functional form, and is then hardened and sloughed off, like antlers or an outgrown shell, but not completely off: it then rotates freely on a lubricated fixed axle. Possible? It's hard to say. Useful? Also hard to say, especially since such a wheel would have to be free-wheeling. This is an interesting speculative exercise, but certainty not one that should inspire us to draw categorical, *a priori* conclusions. It would be foolhardy to declare wheels biologically impossible, but at the same time we can appreciate that they are at least very distant and unlikely solutions to *natural* problems of design.

Now a cognitive wheel is simply any design proposal in cognitive theory (at any level from the purest semantic level to the most concrete level of "wiring diagrams" of the neurons) that is profoundly unbiological, however wizardly and elegant it is as a bit of technology.

Clearly this is a vaguely defined concept, useful only as a rhetorical abbreviation, as a gesture in the direction of real difficulties to be spelled out carefully. "Beware of postulating cognitive wheels" masquerades as good

---

[16] For more details, and further reflections on the issues discussed here, see Diamond (1983).

advice to the cognitive scientist, while courting vacuity as a maxim to follow.[17] It occupies the same rhetorical position as the stockbroker's maxim: buy low and sell high. Still, the term is a good theme-fixer for discussion.

Many critics of AI have the conviction that *any* AI system is and must be nothing but a gearbox of cognitive wheels. This could of course turn out to be true, but the usual reason for believing it is based on a misunderstanding of the methodological assumptions of the field. When an AI model of some cognitive phenomenon is proposed, the model is describable at many different levels, from the most global, phenomenological level at which the behavior is described (with some presumptuousness) in ordinary mentalistic terms, down through various levels of implementation all the way to the level of program code—and even further down, to the level of fundamental hardware operations if anyone cares. No one supposes that the model maps onto the processes of psychology and biology *all the way down.* The claim is only that for some high level of description below the phenomenological level (which merely *sets* the problem) there is a mapping of model features onto what is being modeled: the cognitive processes in living creatures, human or otherwise. It is understood that all the implementation details below the level of intended modelling will consist, no doubt, of cognitive wheels—bits of unbiological computer activity mimicking the gross effects of cognitive sub-components by using methods utterly unlike the methods still to be discovered in the brain. Someone who failed to appreciate that a model composed microscopically of cognitive wheels could still achieve a fruitful isomorphism with biological or psychological processes at a higher level of aggregation would suppose there were good *a priori* reasons for generalized skepticism about AI.

But allowing for the possibility of valuable intermediate levels of modelling is not ensuring their existence. In a particular instance a model might descend directly from a phenomenologically recognizable level of psychological description to a cognitive wheels implementation without shedding any light at all on how we human beings manage to enjoy that phenomenology. I *suspect* that all current proposals in the field for dealing with the frame problem have that shortcoming. Perhaps one should dismiss the previous sentence as mere autobiography. I find it hard to imagine (for what that is worth) that any of the *procedural details* of the mechanization

---

[17] I was interested to discover that at least one researcher in AI mistook the rhetorical intent of my new term on first hearing; he took "cognitive wheels" to be an accolade. If one thinks of AI, as he does, not as a research method in psychology but as a branch of engineering attempting to extend human cognitive powers, then of course cognitive wheels are breakthroughs. The vast and virtually infallible memories of computers would be prime examples; others would be computers' arithmetical virtuosity and invulnerability to boredom and distraction. See Hofstadter (1982) for an insightful discussion of the relation of boredom to the structure of memory and the conditions for creativity.

of McCarthy's circumscriptions, for instance, would have suitable counterparts in the backstage story yet to be told about how human commonsense reasoning is accomplished. If these procedural details lack "psychological reality" then there is nothing left in the proposal that might model psychological processes except the phenomenological-level description in terms of jumping to conclusions, ignoring and the like—and we already know we do that.

There is an alternative defense of such theoretical explorations, however, and I think it is to be taken seriously. One can claim (and I take McCarthy to claim) that while formalizing commonsense reasoning in his fashion would not tell us anything *directly* about psychological processes of reasoning, it would clarify, sharpen, systematize the purely semantic-level characterization of the demands on any such implementation, biological or not. Once one has taken the giant step forward of taking information-processing seriously as a real process in space and time, one can then take a small step back and explore the implications of that advance at a very abstract level. Even at this very formal level, the power of circumscription and the other versions of non-monotonic reasoning remains an open but eminently explorable question.[18]

Some have thought that the key to a more realistic solution to the frame problem (and indeed, in all likelihood, to any solution at all) must require a complete rethinking of the semantic-level setting, prior to concern with syntactic-level implementation. The more or less standard array of predicates and relations chosen to fill out the predicate-calculus format when representing the "propositions believed" may embody a fundamentally inappropriate parsing of nature for this task. Typically, the interpretation of the formulae in these systems breaks the world down along the familiar lines of objects with properties at times and places. Knowledge of situations and events in the world is represented by what might be called sequences of verbal snapshots. State S, constitutively described by a list of sentences true at time t asserting various n-adic predicates true of various particulars, gives way to State', a similar list of sentences true at t'. Would it perhaps be better to reconceive of the world of planning in terms of histories and processes?[19] Instead of trying to model the capacity to *keep track of things* in terms of principles for passing through temporal cross-sections of knowledge expressed in terms of terms (*names* for *things*, in essence) and predicates, perhaps we could model keeping track of things more directly,

---

[18] McDermott 1969 ("A Temporal Logic for Reasoning about Processes and Plans," Section 6, "A Sketch of an Implementation") shows strikingly how many *new* issues are raised once one turns to the question of implementation, and how indirect (but still useful) the purely formal considerations are.

[19] Patrick Hayes has been exploring this theme, and a preliminary account can be found in "Naive Physics 1: The Ontology of Liquids" (Hayes, 1978).

and let all the cross-sectional information about what is deemed true moment by moment be merely implicit (and hard to extract—as it is for us) from the format. These are tempting suggestions, but so far as I know they are still in the realm of handwaving.[20]

Another, perhaps related, handwaving theme is that the current difficulties with the frame problem stem from the conceptual scheme engendered by the serial-processing von Neumann architecture of the computers used to date in AI. As large, fast parallel processors are developed, they will bring in their wake huge conceptual innovations which are now of course only dimly imaginable. Since brains are surely massive parallel processors, it is tempting to suppose that the concepts engendered by such new hardware will be more readily adaptable for realistic psychological modelling. But who can say? For the time being, most of the optimistic claims about the powers of parallel processing belong in the same camp with the facile observations often encountered in the work of neuroscientists, who postulate marvelous cognitive powers for various portions of the nervous system without a clue of how they are realized.[21]

Filling in the details of the gap between the phenomenological magic show and the well-understood powers of small tracts of brain tissue is the immense research task that lies in the future for theorists of every persuasion. But before the problems can be solved they must be encountered, and to encounter the problems one must step resolutely into the gap and ask how-questions. What philosophers (and everyone else) have always known is that people—and no doubt all intelligent agents—can engage in swift, sensitive, risky-but-valuable *ceteris paribus* reasoning. How do we do it? AI may not yet have a good answer, but at least it has encountered the question.[22]

---

[20] Oliver Selfridge's forthcoming monograph, *Tracking and Trailing* (Bradford Books/ MIT Press), promises to push back this frontier, I think, but I have not yet been able to assimilate its messages. There are also suggestive passages on this topic in Ruth Garrett Milliken's *Language, Thought, and Other Biological Categories*, also forthcoming from Bradford Books.

[21] To balance the "top-down" theorists' foible of postulating cognitive wheels, there is the "bottom–up" theorists' penchant for discovering *wonder tissue*. (Wonder tissue appears in many locales. J.J. Gibson's theory of perception, for instance, seems to treat the whole visual system as a hunk of wonder tissue, for instance, resonating with marvelous sensitivity to a host of sophisticated "affordances." See, e.g., J.J. Gibson, 1979.)

[22] One of the few philosophical articles I have uncovered that seem to contribute to the thinking about the frame problem—though not in those terms—is Ronlad de Sousa's "The Rationality of Emotions" (de Sousa, 1979). In the section entitled "What are Emotions For?" de Sousa suggests, with compelling considerations, that:

the function of emotion is to fill gaps left by [merely wanting plus] "pure reason" in the determination of action and belief. Consider how Iago proceeds to make Othello jealous. His task is essentially to direct Othello's attention, to suggest questions to ask . . . Once attention is thus directed, inferences which, before on the same evidence, would not even have been thought of, are experienced as compelling.

REFERENCES

Cherniak, C. (in press). Rationality and the structure of memory. *Synthèse*.

Dennett, D.C. (1978). Two approaches to mental images. *Brainstorms*. Cambridge, MA: MIT Press, A Bradford Book.

Dennett, D.C. (1982a). Why do we think what we do about why we think what we do? *Cognition, 12*, 219–227.

Dennett, D.C. (1982b). How to study consciousness empirically; or, nothing comes to mind. *Synthèse, 53*, 159–180.

Dennett, D.C. (1982c). Beyond belief. In A. Woodfield (Ed.), *Thought and object*. Oxford: Oxford University Press.

Dreyfus, H. (1972). *What computers can't do*. New York: Harper and Row.

Fikes, R., & Nilsson, N. (1971). STRIPS: A new approach to the application of theorem proving to problem solving. *Artificial Intelligence, 2*, 189–208.

Gibson, J.J. (1979). *The ecological approach to visual perception*. London: Houghton Mifflin.

Goodman, N. (1982). Thoughts without words. *Cognition, 12*, 211–217.

Hayes, P.J. (1978). *Naive physics I: The ontology of liquids* (Working Papers No. 35). Geneva, Switzerland: Institut pour les etudes semantiques et cognitives, University of Geneva.

Hayes, P.J. (1979). The naive physics manifesto. In D. Michie (Ed.), *Expert systems in the microelectronic age*. Edinburgh, Scotland: Edinburgh University Press.

Hofstadter, D.R. (1982). Can inspiration be mechanized? *Scientific American, 247*, 18–34.

McCarthy, J. (1960). Programs with common sense. *Proceedings of the Teddington Conference on the Mechanization of Thought Processes*. London: Her Majesty's Stationers Office.

McCarthy, J. (1980, February). *Circumscription—a form of non-monotonic reasoning* (Artificial Intelligence Laboratory Memo AIM-334, p. 4). Stanford, CA: Stanford University.

McCarthy, J., & Hayes, P.J. (1969). Some philosophical problems from the standpoint of artificial intelligence. In B. Meltzer & D. Michie (Eds.), *Machine Intelligence 4*. Edinburgh, Scotland: Edinburgh University Press.

McDermott, D., & Doyle, J. (1980). Non-monotonic logic. *Artificial Intelligence, 13*, 41–72.

Minsky, M. (1981). A framework for representing knowledge. In J. Haugeland (Ed.), *Mind design* (p. 125). Cambridge, MA: MIT Press. A Bradford Book. (Originally published as Memo 3306, Artificial Intelligence Laboratory, Massachusetts Institute of Technology)

In de Sousa's understanding, "emotions are determinate patterns of salience among objects of attention, lines of inquiry, and inferential strategies" (p. 50) and they are not "reducible" in any way to "articulated propositions." Suggestive as this is, it does not, of course, offer any concrete proposals for how to endow an inner (emotional) state with these interesting powers. Another suggestive—and overlooked—paper is Howard Darmstadter's "Consistency of Belief" (Darmstadter, 1971, pp. 301–310). Darmstadter's exploration of *ceteris paribus* clauses and the relations that might exist between beliefs as psychological states and sentences believers may utter (or have uttered about them) contains a number of claims that deserve further scrutiny.

Newell, A. (1982). The knowledge level. *Artificial Intelligence, 18*, 87–127.

Schank, R., & Abelson, R. (1977). *Scripts, plans, goals and understanding: An inquiry into human knowledge structures.* Hillsdale, NJ: Erlbaum.

Selfridge, O. (in press). *Tracking and trailing.* Cambridge, MA: MIT Press. A Bradford Book.

Winograd, T. (1972). *Understanding natural language.* New York: Academic Press.

Woolridge, D. (1963). *The machinery of the brain.* New York: McGraw Hill.

CHAPTER 3

Android Epistemology and the Frame Problem: Comments on Dennett's "Cognitive Wheels"

Clark Glymour

Carnegie-Mellon University, University of Pittsburgh

1. THE FRAME PROBLEM

Dennett (this volume) says the frame problem "is a new, deep epistemological problem—accessible in principle but unnoticed by generations of philosophers—brought to light by the novel methods of AI [artificial intelligence]. . ." Well, yes and no. I think it is more accurate to say that there is no novel problem at all, only a novel and powerful *constraint* on problems that are old friends to philosophy. It's important to see where the novelty is and where it isn't. I think the "frame problem' is not one problem, but an endless hodgepodge of problems concerned with how to characterize what is *relevant* in knowledge, action, planning, etc. Instances of frame problems are all of the form:

Frame Problem Instance: Given an enormous amount of stuff, and some task to be done using some of the stuff, what is the *relevant stuff* for the task?

Most of the instances of this kind that Dennett cites are issues with substantial histories in philosophy, and are not novel at all. What is novel is the constraint I think he imposes on any acceptable answer:

65

Computability Constraint: Any acceptable answer to a frame problem must provide a *feasible algorithm* for computing the relevant stuff in all instances of that problem.

I think Dennett thinks that a further constraint is appropriate on solutions to a frame problem, namely the following one:

Anthropocentric Constraint: Any acceptable answer to a frame problem must provide a feasible algorithm that computes the relevant stuff *in the way people do.*

I want to do four things. First, I want to show that most of the frame problems in Dennett's examples are of a kind that have been considered by philosophers, often for a long while. Second, I want to illustrate the meaning and the power of the Computability Constraint. Third, I will argue that the Anthropocentric Constraint, which is in one way or another presupposed by most philosophical commentators on AI, has two senses, one of them important but vague, the other a Big Mistake. Fourth, since Dennett's practical conclusion is that philosophers ought to take a step towards joining up with AI, I want to say how philosophy and AI together form a subject. I call it Android Epistemology.

2. RELEVANCE AND THE ROBOTS

Dennett describes three robots, all charged with changing things so that they are not blown up by a bomb. All three of them end in a bad way, blown to bits because they fail to solve an instance of a frame problem. The first robot, R1, suffers because he cannot draw consequences. That is partly because he does not know enough and partly because he cannot draw logical consequences of what he knows. The problem for the robot designer is to find a clear formal representation of general knowledge and to characterize entailment within that formulation. The representation must be very detailed and must include a lot of banal knowledge, but other than that the problem is familiar.

Philosophers in this century have mostly thought of the problem of knowledge representation in terms of axiomatizations in formalized languages, and of entailment as either a semantic relation among formal models for the language, or as a corresponding syntactic relation on the formulas of the language. Those sorts of representations, or others that are readily translated into them, are still one of the mainstays of artificial intelligence work on knowledge representation.

The second robot, R1D1, fails to distinguish the relevant consequences of what he knows. He knows enough, and he can infer well enough; he just doesn't infer the right stuff. The design problem is to characterize the relevant consequences of what he knows.

Anderson and Belnap (1975) had a similar problem, and relevance logic was just the result of trying to address it in a general logical setting. One may say that R1D1's problem is different from the problems of logical relevance; it is the problem of characterizing, among the logically relevant consequences of what R1D1 knows, those consequences that are relevant to the robot's interests, assuming R1D1 has an interest in not being blown to bits. If that is not a very common kind of philosophical issue, still a recollection from my wasted youth suggests that it is not really novel. Somewhere (I will never recover the reference, but perhaps it's the *Concluding Unscientific Postscript*) Kierkegaard describes an "objective madman" who has two globes tied to his coattails. Whenever the globes strike one another the madman shouts "Bang! The world is round." Kierkegaard's point is that although the objective madman draws conclusions from what he knows, and the conclusions are perfectly correct and validly drawn, he fails to draw any relevant conclusions. He quite overlooks the conclusions that are salient to life. Kierkegaard's objective madman and Dennett's R1D1 are equally batty, and for the same reason. Similar problems arise in ethics when philosophers are concerned to distinguish the morally relevant consequences of actions.

The third robot, R2D1, has the most interesting problem. He knows how to compute consequences, and for each consequence he knows how to compute whether or not it is relevant. He's blown to bits while computing consequences of what he knows, and computing for each consequence whether it is relevant to his problem. In part, R2D1 is not faced with a new relevance problem, but a characteristic complexity problem about computational constraints, and I will return to it in that context. In part R2D1 has a problem about when to stop gathering information (in this case by drawing consequences and testing them for relevance). The second part of the problem is in a way old hat. Philosophers and economists both know it as the following: When does the expected cost of acquiring further information relevant to a decision problem exceed the expected value of that information?

The robots' frame problems are all familiar philosophical issues, or close enough. The same can be said of a lot of the AI problems that are framish. Perception, learning, planning, and acting generate frame problems, and most of them are of a kind that have been considered one place or another in the philosophical literature.

3. THE COMPUTATIONAL CONSTRAINT

What does the Computational Constraint mean? It doesn't mean merely that an effective procedure must be given for computing the relevant stuff.

The constraint is much more restrictive than that, and it is the additional force of the requirement that may be novel to philosophy.

Dennett's robots all get blown apart because they cannot figure out what to do about the bomb, and do it, at least not rapidly enough. But we could make a robot that wouldn't get blown apart, unlike Dennett's robots. We would simply give our robot, R2D2, a program that specified the right stuff to do for *this bomb in this circumstance.* R2D2's program might direct it, whenever something round with an elongation comes into the viewscreen, to pull the elongation out of the round thing. Aside from the difficulties of computer vision, there is no complexity to that. R2D2 would know how to defuse bombs, and would defuse them. Of course, R2D2 would also pull the stems out of pumpkins, the wicks out of round candles, the penises out of fat men. And if the fusing of the bomb were changed, so that it exploded when pulled, R2D2 would go the same way as Dennett's robots.

Why do we think that R2D2's program is not a solution to the frame problem implicit in Dennett's stories? Roughly, I think, because we have in mind endless variations on the circumstance, and R2D2 would behave inappropriately in most of them. For each specific variation, we can amend R2D2s program so that R2D2 pretty effortlessy takes care of *that* variation, but eventually the variations will grow too large and R2D2 will run out of memory, and there will always be variations for which he fails. Some AI programs look like R2D2's program. There are big collections of knowledge, and fixed connections among the pieces of knowledge, that enable the computer to act as though it knows things and can make inferences. But they contain no adequate general procedure, and when the circumstances are changed a little, they fail. Other AI programs contain general procedures all right, and they run just fine for the cases their authors choose to demonstrate, but their procedures are intractable, and given slightly more complex tasks of the same kind, they fail. These are not solutions to frame problems.

Computation theorists often consider algorithms as effective decision procedures for problems that have infinitely many instances, and that in each instance have either "yes" or "no" as an answer. Thus consider the problem of determining whether a propositional formula is satisfiable. Every well-formed propositional formula is an instance of the problem. The instances can be given a size measured by the length of the formula, and there are only finitely many distinct instances of any given size. There are, of course, algorithms that will solve every instance of the problem. We can measure, in any of a variety of ways, the resources that an algorithm must use to solve a given instance of a problem. Resources can, for example, be measured by the number of steps, or the time, an algorithm requires. For any algorithm that solves a problem, since there are only a finite number of instances of the problem of any given size, n, there is an instance of size n that requires the algorithm to use at least as much time as is required for any other problem instance of size n. We can think of this time, whatever it is, as the *worst case* for problem instances of size n. The algorithm might give an answer in less than this time for some problem instances of size n, but it will never take longer. As n increases, the worst case resource consumption of an algorithm will typically also increase. If the worst case resource consumption is bounded by a polynomial function of the size of the problem instance, the algorithm is said to be feasible. The truth table method for determining the satisfiability of propositional formulae is an effective procedure, but it is not a feasible procedure. The worst case resource requirements increase exponentially with the size of the formula. In fact, no feasible procedure is known for deciding the satisfiability of propositional formulae, or validity, or entailment. It is not just that no one has found a polynomial algorithm that decides satisfiability. Rather, there are thousands of decision problems of interest to computer science for which no polynomial algorithm is known, and if a feasible algorithm for any of these problems, the NP complete problems, could be found, then for each of them there is a feasible algorithm. Satisfiability is an NP complete problem. All of the problems that I will mention later for which no feasible algorithm is known are at least as hard as the NP complete problems. When the Computational Constaint is imposed, none of what philosophers do in logic courses is good enough to answer a frame problem about logical consequences.

There are other ways of measuring complexity, and there are other kinds of problems besides yes–no decision problems for which complexity can be defined. Rather than considering the worst-case complexity of problem instances of size n, we can consider instead the *expected* complexity of problem instances of that size. Expected complexity and worst-case complexity can be very different. For example, the graph 3 coloring problem is the task of deciding for any graph whether all vertices in the graph can be assigned one of three colors in such a way that no pair of adjacent vertices have the same color. No algorithm with polynomial worst case complexity is known, but I am told that the expected complexity is bounded by a constant.[1] Instead of considering algorithms for decision problems that have a yes or no answer, one can consider *search* problems. Instances of search problems ask for a member of a set with some specified property, and an algorithm for a search problem returns for any instance just such a member if there is one, or else the news that there is no such member. We can consider *generation* problems: Given a finite set, generate all of the members of the set with a specified property. Search problems and genera-

---

[1] A fact reported to me by Dale Miller of the University of Pennsylvania.

tion problems can be given a complexity analysis that is similar to the analysis given for decision problems (see Garey & Johnson, 1979; Kelly, 1986).

Return now to Dennett's robots. R1's problem is quite general, and it cannot be solved just by giving the robot a logical theory, or even by giving him a decidable logical theory. If R1 is going to draw consequences of what he knows, he must have a feasible algorithm for doing so, and that means his designers back at the drawing board can't just give him propositional logic.

R1D1 has some feasible procedure for drawing consequences, but no way to determine which of his consequences are relevant to disposing of the bomb. So it looks as though R1D1 needs a feasible algorithm for computing the stuff relevant to avoiding being blown to bits.

R2D1 is the most interesting case, because two problems are involved. R2D1 knows how to compute consequences and, for any consequence, how to compute whether the consequence is relevant. That is already one major problem, as I will explain in a moment. The other problem is that R2D1 has no stopping criterion; he doesn't know when to stop gathering information and take action.

Whether intended or not, R2D1 illustrates an important fact about the Computability Constraint. The way to compute relevant consequences is generally *not* to compute consequences and test them for relevance. The way to compute the relevant members of a collection is generally *not* to test every member of the collection for relevance. The reason is that such strategies require that a lot of things be generated that will in the end be rejected as irrelevant, and thus they waste computational resources. The best solutions to frame problems are algorithms that generate the relevant without ever looking at the irrelevant.

Stopping can be hard because of the Computability Constraint. The algorithm must not look far ahead in deciding whether enough of what is relevant has been computed, because looking ahead requires computation. Somehow, on the basis of what it's got, it must decide when enough is enough.

4. AN EXAMPLE

Consider a simple logical example, which is actually of real practical importance for machine learning. It is taken from the thesis work of my student (and, now, colleague), Kevin Kelly (1986). Suppose we want to design a machine that will form a theory of any domain; in fact, we want it to be able to form a theory of all of the universally valid truths in any domain. The machine is to be given a sequence of facts from the domain, which we can think of as singular sentences, and every fact will eventually be given to it. From the facts the machine is to guess an axiomatization of all of the universal sentences true in the domain. As the evidence changes, the machine can change its guess. The universal sentences true in any domain can be axiomatized by a set of *clauses*, where a clause is simply a universally quantified disjunction of atomic formulae or negations of atomic formulae: "(x)(y)(z)(u)[P(xyz) ∨ Q(xxu)]" might be a clause. (Hereafter, in specifying clauses I will not write down the quantifiers.)

So we can think of the machine's job as that of producing a set of clauses that will entail all of the universal sentences true in the domain. A natural strategy is to guess that the universal sentences true in the domain are just the universal sentences true in the evidence seen so far, or consistent with the evidence seen so far. It can be shown that versions of these strategies will, in a well-defined sense, get the right axiomatization in the limit.

When we say that the machine should proceed by finding an axiomatization of all of the clauses consistent with the evidence it has so far obtained, we have characterized the relevant stuff, and we have addressed the frame problem as a philosopher might. But we have not solved the problem within the requirements of the Computational Constraint. Consider what that constraint means in this context. The machine can search through all of the clauses in the language, testing each of them for consistency with the evidence. It might, for example, start with the simplest and logically strongest universal sentences, e.g., "P(xyz)" and " − Q(xyz)" and test them for consistency with the evidence, and then weaken each clause by identifying some of the variables, e.g., considering "P(xxz)" and "P(xyy)" and " − Q(xyx)" and so on until it gets to formulae such as "P(xxx)" that cannot be further specialized. Then it might go on to disjunctions of clauses we have already considered, e.g., "P(xyz) ∨ − Q(xyx)" and so on.

Quite hopeless. All known algorithms for testing for consistency are worst-case exponential. If we decide nonetheless to do consistency tests, the machine must do as few as possible. Notice that many clauses are logically equivalent: "P(xyy)" is logically equivalent to "P(yyx)". If we have tested the first for consistency with the evidence, there is no need to test the second. So we might hope to avoid consistency tests by first checking to see whether a new clause is logically equivalent to one already considered. That is R2D1's strategy, and it is again quite hopeless. All known algorithms for testing for equivalence of clauses of this kind are worst-case exponential. Somehow we must avoid ever *generating* all those equivalent clauses. Suppose we give each variable a number, say 1 to x and 2 to y and 3 to z and so forth, and consider only clauses in which variable number n occurs before any occurrence of any variable with a number greater than n. So. "P(xyx)" is an admissable clause, but "P(yxy)", though logically equivalent, is not. We lose nothing in expressive power by considering only clauses that meet this requirement, and it can be shown that we reduce exponentially the number of clauses that must be considered. But again, we have only addressed the problem as a philosopher might: We have characterized a sufficient relevant set of things to consider, but we have not provided an algorithm that generates just the admissible clauses. In this case, it turns out, there is a polynomially bounded algorithm that does the job. Suppose we consider a clausal form with 13 variables places, for example, "P(_____) V -R(____) V S(__)" in which no predicate appears twice. Take a vocabulary of 13 variables, and consider all of the ways there are to put some variable in a variable place of this clausal form. The answer is 13^{13} or 302,875,106,592,253. That is how many formulae we would have to generate and test for consistency or equivalence if we searched only this one clausal form without restricting the variable order. Most of these formulae are redundant. If instead we number the 13 variables and generate only admissible clauses, the number is reduced to 27,644,437 formulae, none of which are logically equivalent to any other.

Twenty-seven million and change is still a lot. The savings in computational resources obtained by restricting variable order are not nearly enough for a feasible procedure. We note again that there is no point in considering specializations of clauses that are already known to be consistent with the evidence (for the specializations will necessarily be consistent as well, and they will be entailed by their generalization), and there is likewise no point in considering generalizations of clauses that we know to be inconsistent with the evidence. We can then investigate the possibility of algorithms that avoid considering these unnecessary clauses. What we know about the answers can be found in Kelly (1986).

The fundamental frame problems may not be new, but the kind of work that is needed to solve them in accordance with the Computability Constraint is very new, and very hard.

There is an important limitation on thinking about frame problems under the Computability Constraint, at least as I interpret it. Complexity theory applies to problems that have infinitely many instances, differing in size and difficulty. For any one instance there is always a trivial program that gives the correct answer effortlessly. The situations an android may face are not always (or perhaps often) naturally structured as instances of a general problem to which complexity theory can be applied. An important and neglected part of the philosophical analysis of AI programs and problems consists in locating the particular instances that may be exhibited in an appropriate collection of instances. Further, we may sometimes not care about instances that increase without bound on their size. We are sometimes concerned with algorithms that deal only with finitely many different instances, finitely bounded, but do so without knowing all the answers beforehand. We have as yet no theory for such problems.

5. SCOPE AND THE ANTHROPOCENTRIC CONSTRAINT

What does it mean to require that a solution to a frame problem solve the problem in the way humans do? One thing it might mean is that the artificial intelligence solution must show all of the flexibility and adaptability that humans show.

Consider a human bomb expert. The human bomb expert has a theory about explosives and explosive devices. He can learn about any particular device from information given to him by others, or from tests on the device itself. He can handle endless variations of the situation, and there is no boundary on the information that he can make use of to solve his problem. What we want from a solution to a frame problem is flexibility, not just the ability to handle *bigger* tasks of the same kind, but also tasks that differ in indescribably many ways. Or compare a human chess expert with a chess-playing computer, each playing against a human opponent. The human chess expert can take advantage of his opponent's psychological quirks, he can figure out what distracts or annoys his opponent, he can study his opponent's previous games and form and use a theory about his opponent's weaknesses. He can stop playing chess and play two-move chess problems. He can play three-dimensional chess as soon as he is told the rules. He can play checkers and backgammon and liars' poker and fictionary. He can play chess for fun and chess for blood, real blood. The chess-playing program can't.

There are few contexts in which we have anything like a formal theory of the scope or reliancy or flexibility of an algorithm. Learning is one such context, where there are formal representations of the scope of algorithms for discovering grammars, recursive functions, and first order theories. But we have no theoretical grip on the sort of flexibility at issue with the chess player or the demolitions expert.

The trouble with the Anthropocentric Constraint understood as a demand about flexibility and scope is just that we don't know very well what it means, and we don't know quite how to separate being a flexible chess player from being a flexible game player from being like a human altogether. If the Antropocentric Constraint is taken to mean that a solution to a frame problem must produce behavior that is altogether like a human, then there *is* no frame problem properly within AI: The frame problem just becomes the whole thing, the entire problem of making a computer behave like a human.

6. PSYCHOLOGY AND THE ANTHROPOCENTRIC CONSTRAINT

The other interpretation of the Anthropocentric Constraint is that the algorithms executed by an android in performing a task must, at some appropriate level of description, be the *very same* algorithms that people execute in performing that task. An android that learns language, for example, should learn it through the same computational processes that a child does, right down to the errors and mistakes. The errors children make in forming passive constructions, and plurals, and what have you, should also be the same errors the computer makes.

I can imagine why psychologists should impose this demand. They are, after all, interested in a theory of the computations people execute. But why should anyone interested in *artificial intelligence* want to impose that constraint? I can't for the life of me think of a plausible reason. If the basic assumption of cognitivism in psychology is correct, then human cognition works on computational principles. If that is so, then human cognition is a special case of android epistemology. It is one way, but for all we know *just* one way, of effecting intelligent behavior. If we have some behavior we want a machine to be capable of, and we pretty well know the range and variability of that behavior, and we have a feasible algorithm for carrying it out, why should we add the difficult empirical burden of making sure that the algorithm is the one that runs in people? Why, especially, if the algorithm we have found performs the behavior *better* than people do? I suppose one might believe that the algorithms that run in people will mesh together better than algorithms that don't run in people, and will therefore lead to integrated systems with greater capacity. One might believe it, and of course it might be true, but I don't know of any reason to think so. We don't demand that our pocket calculators emulate human arithmetic errors, and we ought not to make that demand of our vision algorithms, language processing algorithms, learning algorithms, and so on.

7. ANDROID EPISTEMOLOGY

Dennett's real thesis is that there is a lot for philosophers to learn from artificial intelligence, and a lot for them to do that might as well be called artificial intelligence. He's right. There are very hard theoretical problems about what we mean by flexibility and scope, about how to classify problem instances into problems, about how to develop an analysis of complexity for finite numbers of instances, and about how to analyze the complexity of learning problems. There are quite different, but equally hard, questions about how to solve a frame problem, subject to the Computability

Constraint, once a problem is posed. There are problems of characterizing and comparing the possible solutions to a frame problem, or a discovery problem, once it is posed. There is no reason why the tasks considered have to be those that people actually do, or do well. It is enough that they are tasks that people might wish to do, or have an android do, or simply wonder if an android could do.

Philosophical logic and analysis is appropriate for some of these questions, since the relevance problems that arise in AI are generally familiar, but the philosophers' traditional tools are insufficient. The Computational Constraint requires novel and unobvious solutions, and makes everything harder and perhaps more fun.[2]

REFERENCES

Anderson, A., & Belnap, N. (1975). *Entailment.* Princeton, NJ: Princeton University Press.
Garey, M., & Johnson, D. (1979). *Computers and intractability.* San Francisco: Freeman.
Kelly, K. (1986). *Scope and complexity in the automated discovery of universal theories.* Ph.D. thesis, University of Pittsburgh.

------

[2] I thank Kevin Kelly for comments on a draft of this essay.

CHAPTER 4

An Overview of the Frame Problem

John Haugeland

University of Pittsburgh

As if epistemology hadn't enough troubles, artificial inteligence has generously provided another, called the "frame" problem. I hope to explain roughly what this problem is, what it depends on, and what, therefore, it may show.

I will begin with a somewhat unusual perspective, by reviewing some of the prehistory of AI. Aside from early programming aids, the first major effort to use computers for nonmathematical symbol manipulation was *mechanical translation*. Though intermediate goals were discussed, the main target was a machine that could translate arbitrary text from one natural language into another, at the level of competent bilinguals. As a research discipline, "MT" flourished throughout the 1950s, and, at its peak, employed perhaps a thousand specialists, worldwide. The field was more or less launched by a "memorandum," written by Warren Weaver, and sent to about 200 of his friends in 1949.

In this memo (reprinted in Locke & Booth, 1955), Weaver identified multiple word meanings as a crucial problem and proposed to resolve it in terms of the "micro context" surrounding any ambiguous term:

> . . . If one lengthens the slit in [an] opaque mask, until one can see not only the central word in question but also say N words on either side, then if N is large enough one can unambiguously decide the meaning of the central word. The

formal truth of this statement becomes clear when one mentions that the middle word of a whole article or a whole book is unambiguous. . . . The practical question is: What minimum value of N will, at least in a tolerable fraction of cases, lead to the correct choice of meaning for the central word? (p. 21)

Weaver is not terrifically forthcoming about what he expects the machine to do with these contexts; but we get a clue from his remarks about cryptography. He begins by recounting a case in which a message encoded from Turkish was successfully decoded back into Turkish (using statistical techniques) by someone who *knew no Turkish.* (In fact, the decoder didn't recognize the result as a message, and believed he had failed). Weaver goes on to suggest that translation might be regarded as a *species of decoding*[1] and adds:

This approach brings to the foreground an aspect of the matter that probably is absolutely basic—namely, the statistical character of the problem. "Perfect" translation is almost surely unattainable. Processes, which at stated confidence levels will produce a translation which contains only X per cent "error," are almost surely attainable. (p. 22)

Weaver calls this wonderful new approach *statistical semantics;* apparently, the problem of multiple meaning was to be solved by standard cryptographic devices like word frequencies, pair-wise correlations, and so on.

Most astonishingly, there is no mention whatever of trying to *understand* the message; moreover, in this fundamental regard, MT never got beyond Weaver's original version. (Hence, MT is not in any sense artificial intelligence—no "intelligence" was supposed to be involved.) By now, such an approach seems so incredible that we would do well to ponder *why* smart people could take it so seriously for so long. I think something like the following must be right. Before mid-century, the development of many diverse but equivalent notations ("encodings"), for various *formal* languages, had to be fresh in every mathematician's mind; and such systems can be "intertranslated" quite mechanically. Natural languages, of course, are not precisely formal, but they seem to *approximate* formality as an ideal—as if they were genuine formal languages underneath, but somehow sullied by real-world noise and distortion.

Now Weaver himself (along with Claude Shannon) was simultaneously a pioneer in statistical "information theory," one of the prime concerns of

---

[1] He seems to overlook the point that "translate" and "decode" are both used in two ways: (a) figuring out ("cracking") the alien system, leading to a reliable translation manual or key; and (b) using that manual or key to interpret messages as they come in. But, presumably, the main problems of cryptography arise in the former, whereas those of translation arise in the latter.

which is reliable transmission through noisy, distorting channels. Moreover, the basic technique is to introduce a systematic redundancy into the message, which the receiver can later use to eliminate (filter out) channel-induced ambiguity or ellipsis—all this, notoriously, without any attention to what the text might mean. So, why not treat natural language translation just like formal language translation, abetted by modern statistical methods for coping with mundane noise and imperfection? The idea was that "ivory-tower" formalisms could be *generalized* by introducing information-theoretic statistical factors—and that such generalization would capture the vicissitudes of natural language.

The lie to this conception was given by Yehoshua Bar-Hillel, in 1960; he wrote:

> Little John was looking for his toy box. Finally he found it. The box was in the pen. John was very happy.
>
> Assume, for simplicity's sake, that *pen* in English has only the following two meanings: (1) a certain writing utensil, (2) an enclosure where small children can play. I now claim that no existing or imaginable program will allow an electronic computer to determine that the word *pen* in the given sentence within the given context has the second of the above meanings, whereas every reader with a sufficient knowledge of English will do this "automatically." (pp. 159–160)

So much for the symptoms: Bar-Hillel went on to spell out a diagnosis, the necessary therapy, and his own somber prediction:

> What makes an intelligent human reader grasp this meaning so unhesitatingly is. . .his *knowledge* that the relative sizes of pens,. . .[etc.]. "But why not envisage a system which will put this knowledge at the disposal of the translation machine? Understandable as this reaction is, it is very easy to show its futility. What such a suggestion amounts to, if taken seriously, is the requirement that a translation machine should not only be supplied with a dictionary but also with a universal encyclopedia. This is surely utterly chimerical and hardly deserves any further discussion. (pp. 159–160)

Needless to say, artificial intelligence, including a major emphasis on general knowledge representation, has fairly thrived in the decades since that gloomy prognosis. Statistical semantics, however, has quietly disappeared.

I would now *like* to argue that the frame problem does for AI what Bar-Hillel's knowledge problem did for MT—namely, shoot it out of the water —but I don't think I can (quite). The two cases are generically similar in that AI too is deeply inspired by the formalization of logical languages. Hence, we might ask what in the basic conception of artificial intelligence is supposed to capture or accommodate the "informality" of natural language: If AI rejects MT's vision of generalizing the pristine archetype with statistical information theory, what does it propose instead?

Once put, it seems to me that this question actually has an answer, or rather two answers—for, in place of MT's one fundamental intuition, AI substitutes a pair; I call them "internalization" and "control." The idea behind *internalization* is this: If the sequences of utterances in ordinary text and discourse cannot plausibly be regarded as formally "valid," that's because we're only seeing the tips of the icebergs. For various practical reasons, natural language use is wildly enthymematic; many intervening steps and presuppositions are not expressed, but only thought. "Thoughts," of course, are the rest of the iceberg; and the AI suggestion is that natural language will be exposed as a (vast and fancy) formal system after all, once we fill in all the missing pieces.

For instance, in normal communication, many premises may be suppressed, because the receiving system already contains ("knows") them; that implies, however, that some representation of common *knowledge* must be included in the hidden part of the iceberg—the part that AI scientists have to build. (This is what Bar-Hillel foresaw.) Similarly, the sender may suppress "small" steps, including many with commonsense presuppositions, since the receiver can interpolate them more easily than listen to them. But a system that can interpolate formal steps must itself be capable of inferential cognitive processes; that is, natural language use requires *reasoning*. Finally, inasmuch as external and internal representations are subject to different "engineering" constraints, an expressed token need not be the same as its cognitive counterpart, even structurally. Consequently, the systems must support conversion transformations, which may themselves then introduce further abbreviation efficiencies, analogous in principle to the omission of steps and premises—which is to say that decoding an external sentence back into its internal form is a nontrivial process, tantamount to *understanding* the sentence.

The internalization move, however, raises the stakes for AI, as compared to MT. A mechanical translation system need cope only with the steps actually present on the page, handling uncertainties statistically. An artificial intelligence, by contrast, with most of the conversation internal and unsaid, must generate the intervening components as needed—it has to think for itself. The new problem then is: *What* should it think? In a typical logical system, subsequent steps are constrained by previous ones, but seldom uniquely determined. Hence, something else has to determine which premises actually get invoked, and which inferences get drawn. In other words, over and above an internal formal language, a functioning AI system also needs some determinate *control*, to guide and choose the actual processes in real time. Recognizing and addressing this requirement is AI's second basic "generalization" of traditional formal languages.

There have been many approaches to thought control in artificial intelligence; it suffices to mention a couple of the most prominent. One, of course, is the imposition of explicit guidelines, called *heuristic rules*. Heuristics are typically conceived as rather broad choice or evaluation procedures that might be brought to bear on any number of distinct questions; so, they are like commonsense "how to solve it" maxims. It turns out, however, that such general-purpose rules are seldom sufficient by themselves, except in restricted puzzle cases.

Another way of guiding or affecting the direction of a system's processing is by prestructuring the set of alternatives from which it will select, such that desirable options are easy to find. Thus, it is well known that the same problem can be formulated in ways corresponding to quite different "problem spaces," and that these differences greatly affect problem difficulty. A cross-referenced knowledge base, such as a semantic net, a hierarchical record tree, or what have you, is essentially a search space with a structure imposed on it by the cross-linkages. The advantage of such a space is that the local structure is highly flexible and can be explicitly "customized" to the contents of individual nodes—so that even fairly simple heuristics can find their way around efficiently. Insofar as the issues in knowledge representation concern the organization and internal structure of a body of knowledge (as opposed to its contents), they are addressing the problem of real-time control in AI.

We can illustrate how both internalization and control work by sketching an AI treatment of Bar-Hillel's box-in-the-pen example. Disambiguating "pen" requires access to the system's handy knowledge base—facts about typical sizes, for example. Obtaining and using such information is the sort of thing I meant by intervening steps involving hidden premises. Trouble is, common sense "knows" a lot; and the problem with that is not storage capacity, but access time: *finding* what you need, when you need it. Thus, you better not be distracted by all you know about carburetors and cactus flowers on the way to realizing that a toybox probably wouldn't fit in a fountain pen (or you won't get there in time). But how could a system tell (efficiently) that size is the critical factor, and then how can it find the particular sizes it needs?

A popular suggestion (with many variants) is that knowledge be organized in conceptual "clusters," or *stereotypes*, each containing a bunch of common information about some familiar item or situation. In the case at hand, the system might invoke four stereotypes, cued by the words in the sentence: one each for "box" and "in," and two for "pen." Though these will include numerous assorted facts, the "in" stereotype will conspicuously list a prerequisite: its first argument must be smaller in size than its second. Alerted by this explicit requirement, the system will promptly check the typical-size entries in the other three stereotypes—and resolve the ambiguity without further ado. The essential efficiency is in keeping the system from even glancing at a zillion irrelevant inferences on which it could easily waste time. This is what I meant by "controlling" the processing—in this case, almost entirely by virtue of knowledge organization.

> Once upon a time, there were three boxes: Papa box, Mama box, and little Baby box. Papa box was resting on the floor in the middle of their modest cottage, with Baby box perched up on his back; meanwhile, Mama box was sitting quietly on a chair over by the door. Suddenly, in rolls Goldiwires, bent on problem solving. Slowly and carefully, she shoves Papa box across the room to the opposite wall.
>
> *Tough question:* How many boxes are there now?

Well, what's so hard about that? The number of boxes obviously doesn't change; so why doesn't the robot just "remember?" Lots of things, however, *do* change—some manifest, some not. First, of course, when Goldy pushes Papa around, both their locations change—which shouldn't be too hard to anticipate, since it's more or less built into the notion of "shoving." The trouble is, these "direct" consequences also have *side effects* that are not built into shoving as such; thus, in the above situation, Baby will go along for the ride. As a result, whenever Goldy acts, she has to "update" a variety of her other situational beliefs; and the question then arises: *Which* beliefs need to be reconsidered, and which need not? How can she know, for instance, to revise Baby's position, while not bothering to recount boxes? This is the *frame problem* (as first noted and named by McCarthy & Hayes, 1969).

How is it different from the box/pen example? The fundamental difference is the introduction of a *time* parameter. Thus, our stereotype treatment of boxes in pens was essentially timeless: The facts used, about sizes and prerequisites, are all constant—the system needn't reconfirm that pens are *still* only a centimeter thick. When things start moving around, on the other hand, propositions that were once true may not stay that way; hence, if you're counting on some "fact" at some time, you have to make sure it hasn't changed since you last knew it. It seems, then, that the system's knowledge must be divided into (at least) two categories: *perennial* facts that stay the same and *temporary* facts that are subject to change (those that constitute the "present" situation).

The frame problem arises in keeping temporary knowledge up to date, when there are side effects; more specifically, it concerns how a system can *ignore* most conceivable updating questions and confront only "realistic" possibilities. In this respect, the frame problem is analogous to the knowledge access problem, addressed by stereotypes; in both cases, the issue is how to "home in on" relevant considerations, without wasting time on everything else the system knows. Thus, the challenge is not how to decide for each fact whether it matters, but rather how to *avoid* that decision for almost every bit of knowledge. But the two problems are not the same and for two (connected) reasons. First, when accommodating changes, the system must not only find its way around the knowledge base, but also question much of what it discovers there and selectively update the entries. Second, these update decisions are themselves "situation bound"; that is, the actual side effects of any particular event will be quite sensitive to the details of the current situation—hence, generic or "precanned" responses aren't reliable.

Standard approaches to the frame problem can be divided into two main camps, which I call, respectively, the "cheap test" and "sleeping dog" schools.[2] The difference between the two turns on how seriously they mean "ignore." The *cheap test* strategy looks over everything quickly, to tell "at a glance" most of what's irrelevant (hence unchanged). The basic intuition is easy to see in examples: When Goldy pushes Papa, she knows that various positions may change, but she also knows that none of those changes will affect anybody's color, or mass, or shape, or what have you—because (under normal circumstances) position, color, mass, shape, and so on, are *independent* characteristics. Thus, all she needs is a prior *categorization* of events and facts, based on which types of events affect which types of facts. Then each fact-entry in a situation model can fly a conspicuous "flag," indicating the category(ies) of events that might affect it. So, for instance, if a position-affecting event occurs, she can pass over all facts except those flying red flags (which mark position-sensitive items), thereby avoiding lots of irrelevant reconsideration.

In a similar spirit, Goldy can generally assume that only things in the "vicinity" of an event will be affected. Thus, Baby might well be influenced by Papa's move (because he's right there); but Mama and the chair won't be bothered, because they're nowhere near. In this version, the "flags" would represent not property interaction, but object interaction, according to some measure of causal proximity. Either way, however, the system must scan the entire model, relying on some easy sign to rule out most entries without further examination; and that's what I mean by a "cheap test."

The trouble with cheap tests, as you might have guessed, is that the world isn't as nicely structured as all that. In the real world, Mama might very well be affected if Goldy starts messing with Papa; and the alterations might very well include color and shape. Moreover, the potential for these variations to affect other properties of other objects is almost unlimited; and further examples abound. Of course, the tests could be made more discriminating, with additional conditions and qualifications; but then they're no longer cheap, which was the whole point.

---

[2] A much more careful survey of the problem and its literature is contained in an excellent article (this volume) by Lars-Erik Janlert, "Modeling Change—The Frame Problem."

The alternative, *sleeping dog*, strategy is to let everything lie, unless there's some positive reason not to. That is, unless there's some positive indication that a particular fact may be affected, the system will *totally* ignore it, without even performing any cheap tests. This is a satisfying suggestion on the face of it; but it raises formidable design questions about how to get the needed "positive indications" for all the important side effects. How, for instance, will it occur to the system that it better worry about Baby's future position (though not Mama's) when it starts moving Papa? I will mention two ideas that have some currency and power.

One proposal is to divide all temporary facts further into *basic* and *nonbasic* facts, such that (a) non-basic facts are all derivable from basic facts, and (b) basic facts are all independent of one another. The hope, in other words, is to confine side effects to nonbasic facts—that is, to "complexes" of basic facts, as expressed in their consequences. A perfect example is a chessboard: Positions of the individual pieces are basic, and all other facts (threats, vulnerabilities, advantages, etc.) are derivative.[3] Given such a division, it suffices to decompose defined events into their basic constituents (i.e., alterations in basic facts), and then update only what is specified in the definitions. Since the basic facts are independent, nothing else basic changes; so the "basic" frame problem disappears.

That leaves only nonbasic facts to deal with; and, indeed, only *explicitly noted* nonbasic facts are an issue. Thus, any decent set of basic facts will have untold numbers of tedious logical consequences; and no robot in its right mind would actually derive all (or even very many) of them. So most nonbasic facts remain implicit, and these are no problem: No sooner are the basic facts updated than all their implicit consequences are updated too, at the very speed of logic. Still, at least some nonbasic facts must be derived explicitly; and these beliefs are then in danger of having the rug pulled out from under them, whenever a basic fact is updated. One brutally direct response is simply to throw out all explicit inferences, whenever anything is updated; but that's clearly wasteful. A subtler approach associates with each basic fact all the explicit conclusions that depended on it; then the system can tell which beliefs are in jeopardy at any update, and safely ignore the others.

Philosophers, however, will be unsurprised (and perhaps secretly gratified) to learn that computer scientists have had trouble picking out just which facts are basic. If Mama's and Papa's positions are basic, for example, then moving Papa won't affect Mama; and the changing distance and direction between them will be nicely derivative—just like on a chessboard.

---

[3] The basic facts are independent not in the sense that all possible combinations are actually allowed, but only in the sense that if any allowed change is made, no other basic facts are thereby altered. Thus, it's not allowed to put two chess pieces on one square, nor to move the king into check; but when any piece moves, the others stay put.

But, by the same reasoning, Baby's position should be basic too, in which case it won't be affected by Papa's move either; thus, when Papa goes, Baby stays behind, awkwardly suspended in thin air. Well, why not make each object's position basic *relative to* what supports it? Then, Baby's position relative to Papa would remain unchanged when Papa moves, which seems right. But what if Baby is also tied to the doorknob with a string? Or, what if, instead of sliding sideways, Papa tips over? Then Baby's position relative to Papa doesn't seem so "basic" after all; and other suggestions have comparable problems. Moreover, the Boxes' frugal cottage isn't much more complicated than a chessboard; delineating basic facts in, say, a suburban kitchen would be noticeably harder.

The other main variant of the sleeping dog strategy attempts to embrace these interdependent "what ifs" of everyday life in complicated commonsense definitions, essentially like stereotypes. Thus, included within the "move something" stereotype would be a clause pointing out that anything supported by what moves will come along for the ride, . . . unless it's roped to the doorknob, assuming the support doesn't tip over, so long as there are no low bridges, and so on. Of course, these hedges will themselves need to be qualified, in case Baby is glued to Papa, the doorknob is glued to Papa, or whatever. Needless to belabor, such stereotypic definitions could get *very* messy—raising the worry that the frame problem is not such much resolved as relocated, in the problem of finding one's way around the stereotypes themselves.

We can pursue that worry by thinking a little further about stereotypes. Compare horses and living rooms. With rare exceptions, horses all have legs, ears, and tails; they contain blood, bones, and stomachs; they can be used for riding and pulling plows. Living rooms, likewise, have many things in common: By and large, they have walls, windows, and ceilings; they typically contain soft chairs, low tables, and rugs; they can be used for loud parties or quiet conversations. It looks as if we have stereotypes for both.

But the cases are not really comparable. Horses not only have legs; they have exactly four legs, which, moreover, are a matched set, attached in standard locations; their bones are always arranged in a standard equine skeleton; and there are, after all, rather few ways to ride a horse. Living rooms, by contrast, can have any number of windows, in any number of locations; the furniture, not to mention its arrangement, varies enormously from one room to the next, and it often doesn't match; finally, there are all kinds of ways to have a loud party or a quiet conversation. The point is that living rooms differ far more than horses do—particularly at an "intermediate" level of detail—and current *situations* differ even more than the rooms they (sometimes) occur in.

That means that stereotypes for situations (or for changes in situations) cannot possibly have the same kind of determinate, reliable specificity that can be expected of stereotypes for horses (fountain pens, etc.). Either they must disregard middle-level detail (mention the furniture and windows, but say nothing about what they're like or where), or else they must leave lots of open slots or "variables," to be filled in with specifics on each occasion. In the former case, the frame problem is not addressed, because side effects are strongly conditioned by situation-specific details: Is Baby resting on Papa (*this time*), or on the table next to him? On the other hand, if the crucial details are left as variables to be assigned, then there must be some mechanism for making and *updating* these assignments: When Papa moves, how are the slot-holders for the living room stereotype to be readjusted? In other words, the frame problem just reappears in the guise of "applying" stereotypes concretely, in real time.

Imagine that, instead of a *description* of the Boxes' cottage, no matter how elaborate and comple, Goldiwires's head actually contains a miniature *scale model*, complete with tiny ropes, tiny doorknobs, and what have you. In this system, a representation of X's motion is a motion of X's representation; thus, for Goldiwires to represent herself shoving Papa (whether with conviction or just in imagination) is for her little self-model to roll over and shove the little Papa-model, in the corresponding direction. And the beauty of it is that all the side effects take care of themselves: if the Baby model is perched atop the Papa model, then it will come along for the ride—unless it's tied to the tiny doorknob with the tiny rope, and so on. Put more generally, representations of side effects of events are just side effects of the representations of those events. So, the frame problem seems solved for free; . . . a little *too* free, one suspects.

Not wanting to be thieves, we cautiously decline to endorse scale models as mental representations; rather, we begin our honest toil by asking *why* they *seem* so potent against the frame problem. What, in other words, is saliently different about this kind of representation, as compared to something broadly linguistic in inspiration? Note first that we won't get much help from the analog/digital distinction, at least in the tradition of continuous "flow" versus discrete "click-stops." There's no obvious principled reason why scale models couldn't be just as effective if they were discretely "digitized" (like wirephotos, say); hence, digital computers *as such* aren't the crucial issue, either.

The original "analogy" idea in 'analog', however, is not so quickly dismissed; for the standard, all too familiar, contrast between depictive and descriptive modes of representation, between graven images and articulate propositions, is that the former *resemble* their objects, whereas the latter represent only via *arbitrary conventions*. Thus, the miniature Papa represents the real one by having the same shape and coloration, as well as a corresponding size and location, relative to the rest of the model. The *name* 'Papa', on the other hand, represents Papa merely by stipulation—any other name could have been used just as easily. Unfortunately, difficulties emerge when we try to spell out what this contrast really means.

In the first place, a wire-photo represents its object depictively, even when it's a stream of pulses zipping across the Atlantic or stored on magnetic tape. One (oblique) reason for accepting this is that converting between tape-recorded "images" and ordinary visible ones is conceptually straightforward and semantically neutral; that is, it's quite on a par with the conversion between magnetically encoded text and old-fashioned typescript. But converting between depictive images (in either form) and descriptive text (in either form) is a profound problem, nowhere near solved, and not at all semantically neutral; that is, pattern recognition is hard, and almost certainly requires rich knowledge of the objects represented.

On the face of it, however, taped pulse streams don't much *resemble* their objects; it takes a complicated rigmarole to relate them to the "scene" depicted: four pulses for the brightness of each dot, say, and a thousand dots per raster line. Here's the rub: this fancy protocol is just as conventional and arbitrary as the syntax and vocabulary of any language. Of course, once the system is established, then the representation of a given situation is not arbitrary; but the same goes for description. Thus the intuitive clarity of the distinction between conventional symbol schemes and "natural" simulacra begins to cloud up—which is not to say that it isn't still there, but only that it's not so easy to see.

Psychologist Stephen Palmer suggests that "propositional" systems are distinguished as follows: In addition to the representational "elements" that stand for objects, there are further *separate* elements standing for the properties and relations of those objects. (Palmer, 1978. My attention was directed to this article by Janlert's paper, this volume.) The alternative is to let properties and relations of objects be represented, not by additional elements, but by properties and relations of the elements standing for the objects. Thus, if we represent the fact that Papa is big by writing his name in big (or bright red) letters, then that's *not* propositional, because no new item is introduced; but, if we represent the same fact by relating Papa's name to a further element—e.g., a circle drawn around it, or a token of "is-big" after written it—then that *is* propositional. Likewise, we might represent Papa and Mama as married by writing their names next to each other, or in a single type font (nonpropositional), or by writing their names with a single line drawn beneath them, or a token of "is-married-to" between them (propositional).

Now I take it as grounds for suspicion whenever a metaphysical principle hinges on the difference between italics and underlining. Suppose our representation of Papa is a cartoon drawing, with a black outline and a colored interior. Is that one element with a color property, or two elements related by containment? Would it matter if the black and colored parts were in separate layers of a photographic emulsion? Would it matter if the color were paint adhering directly to the surface of a wooden Papa-model? More generally, why isn't "being printed to the left of a token of 'is-big'" a *property* of a token of 'Papa'?[4]

But Palmer (1984) is out for bigger game: Propositions, he says, represent properties and relations *extrinsically*, whereas scale models and their ilk represent properties and relations *intrinsically* (pp. 270–274, 294–299).

> Representation is (purely) intrinsic whenever a representing relation has the same inherent constraints as its represented relation. That is, the logical structure required of the representing relation is intrinsic to the relation itself rather than imposed from outside. (p. 271)

Palmer mainly considers simple comparative relations, like taller- or longer-than; but I prefer (for reasons that will emerge) to begin with a richer domain. Accordingly, suppose we need to keep tabs on the spatial relations among BMW garages in Saudi Arabia. One obvious approach is to put little blue dots on a map of Arabia, letting interdot distances and directions represent corresponding intershop relations. An equally obvious alternative is to state each distance-and-direction relation explicitly, in a list of sentences, or a large chart.

Spatial relations in Arabia obey a number of rigid constraints, as spelled out in geometry and trigonometry. With the map system, the represented distances and directions, whether accurate or not, at least cannot help but accord with all those constraints. For instance, there is no way to represent three garages as being at the vertices of a triangle violating the Pythagorean theorem, the constraints inherent in the representational medium itself prevent such a representation. With a set of sentences, on the other hand, it's all too easy to describe an impossible situation:

Aba 100-miles-north-of Aca.
Aba 200-miles-northwest-of Ada.
Aca 600 miles-west-of Ada.

Of course, we might know better, and carefully avoid such infelicities; but that's just what Palmer means by "imposing" constraints from outside. Thus, the list represents the distances and directions *extrinsically*, while the map represents them *intrinsically*.

---

[4] Wilfrid Sellars, in fact, has proposed (1984) a theory of predication, according to which *linguistic* predicates are essentially just elaborate and versatile typeface markers—that is, "auxilliary symbols" that serve, like underlines, to give individual constants (e.g., names) different *properties*.

The example, however, has a fatal flaw: It trades on a hidden variable, which, when exposed and "controlled for," destroys the result. Each dot on the map represents the position of *one* shop, individually and separately. But each entry in the list gives the relative distance and direction between *two* shops. Thus, the hidden variable is whether the basic representations are monadic or dyadic—one shop or two. And we control for that variable by reversing it in the respective schemes. Thus, a dyadic map-like scheme takes shops two at a time, and represents the distance and direction between them by the distance and direction between two *otherwise isolated* dots. Hence, only relative information is available in each pair; and then it's easy to violate all the constraints:

Aba * Aca *	* Aba * Ada

Aca *	* Ada

On the other hand, a list can easily be constructed, stating the individual location of each garage in Cartesian coordinates; and, then try as you might, you will never be able to describe a configuration violating the Pythagorean theorem, or any of the other constraints. (Essentially the same criticism applies to Palmer's own simpler examples.)

The monadic/dyadic contrast, however, cannot be the root of the matter; for monadic "absolute" positions are nothing other than *relative* displacements from a *common* origin. What really makes the above incoherent representations possible is not their being dyadic, but their being *redundant*. Thus, if you represent Aba (or the origin) as 100 miles north of Aca and also 200 miles northwest of Ada, then there is no need to further specify the Aca–Ada relation—for it is already implicit in the first two claims. If you go ahead and specify some Aca–Ada relation anyway, then that redundant specification can conflict with what was previously implicit; hence, incoherence is possible. The "monadic" schemes indirectly prevent this eventuality, by requiring that one term of the relation always be the origin (which is just enough to rule out redundancy).

Still, maps *are* different from lists of propositions; and we'd like to know how. I think the following is important. Imagine "combining" representations of the Aba–Aca and the Aba–Ada relations, so that they use a single token for the common term, Aba. Thus, we would get composite *propositional* representations like:

Aba is 100 miles north of Aca *AND* 200 miles northwest of Ada and composite *map-style* representations like:

Aba *

Aca *

* Ada

In both cases, the Aca–Ada relation is also "determined," but the contrast is manifest. In the compound proposition, there remains a clear and sharp difference between the initial two *explicit* representations, and the resulting *implicit* one: It would take some calculation to get the latter on a par with the former. In the composite map, on the other hand, there is no such distinction: The Aca–Ada representation is already exactly on a par with the other two. Indeed, there's no way to tell which two relations were given initially, and which emerged therefrom.

More generally, the explicit/implicit distinction appears to collapse for maps and scale models. For instance, many "higher" spatial features of the Arabian landscape—colinearity, betweenness, shape, etc.—would also remain implicit in a list of locations (or cause redundancy, if spelled out); on a map, however, such features are just as "immediately" represented as the individual locations, or pairwise relations. This seeming directness of map-like representation is reminiscent of *explicit* statements, in that nothing has to be figured out or inferred from something else. On the other hand, if the location of one garage on a map is changed, then all the represented relationships involving that garage are *ipso facto* updated too. And this is reminiscent of our earlier remark about *implicit* consequences—that they are updated automatically, at the very speed of logic. The point, therefore, is not that quasi-pictorial representations are all explicit or all implicit, but rather that they are neither. The explicit/implicit distinction itself seems only to make sense for quasi-linguistic ("propositional") representations, with their associated notion of inference.

With nary a hint of whimsy, we might coin a new descriptive term, and call quasi-pictorial representations *complicit*—thereby inviting ourselves eventually to formulate and address various follow-up questions about what we meant. In the meantime, it suffices to note that "complicity" (whatever exactly it amounts to) seems closely relevant to the frame problem. For, the central difficulty is a dilemma: (a) in a quasi-linguistic system, only explicit representations are immediately usable—implicit consequences must be explicitly inferred before they can make any difference to anything; yet (b) once a consequence is explicitly drawn out, it is no longer "automatically updated" when other representations are changed—explicit representations are all quite independent of one another. "Complicit" representations, however, appear to avoid this dilemma: In some sense, everything is directly available, and yet, when one aspect is altered, anything that depends on it is updated automatically too. I think this is what makes the scale model in Goldy's head look so enticing, *prima facie.*

The lesson here (if any) is that the frame problem may be an artifact of certain theoretical assumptions—specifically, the selection of a certain general form or kind of representation. If the problem arises only when there is an explicit/implicit distinction, and if not all representational systems support such a distinction, then, presumably, some representational systems would avoid the problem entirely. Therefore, the frame problem may indirectly contribute to (or constrain) discussions of mental representation.

It is all too tempting, in this context, to think of *mental images.* Of course, it is still controversial whether there really are any "imagistic" mental representations or processes; but my own (outsider's) impression is that the experiments keep pointing in that direction—and that explaining them away is getting harder and harder. In fact, if there are no mental images, then I think nature is guilty of a cunningly orchestrated conspiracy to mislead us on the point.

Imagistic representations, however, are no panacea. Recall that we began our little fantasy not with an image in Goldy's head, but with a *scale model.* The difference matters. When some of the dots on a map get shifted around, the others aren't really affected: Nothing "happens" to them—they just stand in altered geometric relations to the ones that moved. But when the tiny Papa model slides across the floor in the scale cottage, the Baby model is itself actually transported; it is physically carried along. In other words, not only are geometric relations in the world mimicked by geometric relations in the representation, but also *causal* relations in the world are mimicked by causal relations in the model. Moreover, this duplication of the causal structure is crucial to the original seductive formula: Representations of the side effects of a change ought to be side effects of the representation of that change—hence "automatic," "free," and so on.

To be sure, literal *duplication* is not really required (even in miniature). Mental images, after all, are not supposed to be little *pictures* that you could cut out and carry in your wallet, or even that a neurosurgeon could peek in on, or photograph. Rather, they need only be physically instantiated in some way or other such that they can "act" or "function" like images, in an appropriate "processing" environment. Now, what exactly that means is the sixty-four dollar question—the very one that distinctions like Palmer's intrinsic versus extrinsic, and my complicit versus implicit/explicit, are struggling to illluminate. But whatever the ultimate formulation, it should apply to causal as well as to geometric relationships. In other words, the causal structure need only be represented intrinsically, or complicitly, or something like that, and not literally replicated inside the brain.

Alas, to my knowledge, none of the now fairly voluminous mental-image research suggests anything of the sort—that is, there are no mental scale models, complete with automatic causal side effects. On the other hand, I can think of no obvious reason why there couldn't be such things; so, maybe somebody who knows how should look for some.

I would like to conclude with a rather different observation. It seems to me that published examples of the frame problem show a striking lack of diversity: Basically, they all consist of one object hauling, shoving, or deflecting another, with the crudest bump-and-grind sort of causal interaction. Moreover, it's not easy to come up with different examples—which raises an interesting question: Why should this be?

As with many issues in artificial intelligence, human beings *de facto* set the standard for the frame problem. Not only must a clear example of the problem include causal side effects that are not easy to anticipate in a quasi-linguistic model, but also these effects must be ones that any sensible *person* would "see" right away. The hard part is not just finding examples of obscure side effects, but finding ones that people nevertheless instantly appreciate. Now, explaining *that* fact is a problem for theoretical psychology, and therefore provokes wild speculation.

Here's mine. One thing that's frightening about "mental scale models" is that there's no obvious end to them: Why not just recreate the entire universe, monad-like, inside each individual brain? Well, because it's manifestly absurd, that's why. But what could motivate, or even delineate a more modest scheme? Jerry Fodor (1983) has argued that the mind comprises a number of independent and highly specialized "peripheral" subsystems, each of which is incredibly good at one very important job, and no good at anything else. Syntactical parsing is one candidate task for such a dedicated processor; face recognition is another; and image scanning and rotation are yet a third. So, why not imagine a special subsystem dedicated to complicit representation of simple bump-and-grind causal dependencies among salient objects in a situation? (Possibly this would just be a further aspect of the subsystem that also handles image manipulation.) If such a facility is feasible at all, it would account nicely for our own otherwise quite remarkable immunity to the frame problem; and, in the meantime, there would be no difficulty in concocting evolutionary rationales for why it should exist.

What would all this do for AI? The main suggestion is that the frame problem may be an artifact of assuming that mental representation is quasi-linguistic. Since, however, that is one of the basic enabling assumptions of "classical" artificial intelligence (what I earlier called the internalization move), there seems little room for compromise: Perhaps the frame problem is really a "pseudo problem," foisted on unsuspecting epistemology by misguided presumptions underlying AI as a discipline. Even so, the consequences might be disappointingly limited. If the resolution is some special "scale model" peripheral, complicitly representing a few conspicuous causal dependencies, then AI would indeed be blown out of that part of the water. But "central" cognitive processes remain untouched by such speculation; accordingly, they are still anybody's game.

REFERENCES

Bar-Hillel, Y. (1960). The present status of automatic translation of languages. In F.L. Alt (Ed.), *Advances in computers* (pp. 159–160). New York: Academic Press.

Fodor, J. (1983). *The modularity of mind.* Cambridge, MA: MIT Press, A Bradford Book.

McCarthy, J., & Hayes, P. (1969). Some philosophical problems from the standpoint of artificial intelligence. In B. Meltzer & D. Michie (Eds.), *Machine Intelligence 4.* Edinburgh, Scotland: Edinburgh University Press.

Palmer, S. (1978). Fundamental aspects of cognitive representation. In E. Rosch & B. Lloyd (Eds.), *Cognition and categorization* (pp. 294f.). Hillsdale, NJ: Erlbaum.

Sellars, W. (1983). Toward a theory of predication. In J. Bogen & J. McGuire (Eds.), *How things are.* Dordrecht, Netherlands: Reidel.

Weaver, W. (1955). Translation. In W. Locke & D. Booth (Eds.), *Machine translation of language.* Cambridge, MA: MIT Press.

CHAPTER 5

How to Stop Worrying about the Frame Problem Even though It's Computationally Insoluble

Hubert L. Dreyfus
Stuart E. Dreyfus

University of California, Berkeley

As time passes and/or actions are performed, many facts change but not all facts change and only a few such changes are relevant to current action. If one is interested in representing everyday knowledge, this basic characteristic of the everyday world raises a serious problem. The frame problem, as this problem has come to be called, has been defined as "the problem of finding a representational form permitting a changing, complex world to be efficiently and adequately represented" (Janlert, this volume). Daniel Dennett (this volume, p. 130) has called the frame problem "a new, deep epistemological problem—accessible in principle but unnoticed by generations of philosophers—brought to light by the novel methods of AI, and still far from being solved" and Jerry Fodor sees in the frame problem a holistic problem which cognitive science has no idea how to solve.

> [A]s soon as we begin to look at cognitive processes other than input analysis ... we run into problems that have a quite characteristic property. They seem to involve... computations that are, in one or other respect, sensitive to the whole belief system... In this respect, it seems to me, the frame problem is

paradigmatic, and in this respect the seriousness of the frame problem has not been adequately appreciated. (Fodor, 1983, pp. 113–115)

Both Dennett and Fodor find hints of the frame problem in *What Computers Can't Do* (Dreyfus, 1979). Dennett calls it "the smoking pistol [Dreyfus] was looking for but didn't *quite* know how to describe" (Dennett, this volume). And Fodor comments: "If someone—a Dreyfus, for example—were to ask us why we should even suppose that the digital computer is a plausible mechanism for the simulation of global cognitive processes, the answering silence would be deafening" (pp. 126–129). However, while both Fodor and Dennett have highlighted serious difficulties for AI, neither Dennett nor Fodor, nor Dreyfus for that matter, have so far homed in on the frame problem. As we shall see, Dennett's account of the frame problem is indistinguishable from the more general problem of storing and accessing commonsense knowledge, while Fodor identifies the frame problem with two different problems, one too simple to count as the frame problem, since it could be solved by frames, and the other more difficult than the frame problem, the general problem of relevance.

Dennett (this volume) illustrates what he takes to be the frame problem as follows:

> The frame problem is rather like the unsettling but familiar "discovery" that so far as armchair thought can determine, a certain trick we have just observed is flat impossible.
>
> Here is an example of the trick...How is it that I can get myself a midnight snack?...I'll just go and check out the fridge, get out the requisite materials, and make myself a sandwich, to be washed down with a beer....
>
> Now of course I couldn't do this without knowing a good deal—about bread, spreading mayonnaise, opening the fridge, the friction and inertia that will keep the turkey between the bread slices and the bread on the plate as I carry the plate over to the table beside my easy chair. I also need to know about how to get the beer out of the bottle into the glass. Thanks to my previous accumulation of experience in the world, fortunately, I am equipped with all this worldly knowledge....We know trillions of things; we know that mayonnaise doesn't dissolve knives on contact, that a slice of bread is smaller than Mount Everest, that opening the refrigerator doesn't cause a nuclear holocaust in the kitchen.
>
> There must be in us—and in any intelligent agent—some highly efficient, partly generative or productive system of representing—storing for use —all the information needed.

This problem of how to store and access trillions of facts is too static to be the frame problem. But, in any case, what this description of a bit of everyday activity shows is that if we construe our everyday understanding as based on knowledge of facts, our everyday skills look like impossible feats.

Dennett (this volume) asks: "Do we have any model for how such unconscious information-appreciation might be accomplished?" and answers quite lucidly: "The only model we have *so far* is *conscious*, deliberate information-appreciation. Perhaps, AI suggests, this is a good model. If it isn't, we are all utterly in the dark for the time being" (p. 137). So Dennett accepts the AI line: all intelligent behavior must somehow involve processing *elements* of information *about* the world: knowing-how must be explained in terms of knowing *that*. Thus all intelligent *doing* is assumed to involve *thinking*. When Dennett is describing his know-how for pouring beer into a glass he says ". . . I need to know *about* [italics added] how to get the beer out of the bottle" . . . (p. 134). Why not just *know how* to get it out? Presumably because, according to Dennett, in doing psychology, "one reasons about what the agent must *"know"* or *figure out* [italics added] *unconsciously* or *consciously* in order to perform in various ways" (p. 135).

This way of describing everyday skills turns them into a sort of problem-solving—a description which would be appropriate if the beer were frozen so I needed to call up all I knew about ice, and bottles, etc., in order to figure out how to get the beer out of the beer bottle. Since only in such problem situations do we normally stop and notice what we are doing, it may seem that we are always performing such deliberations—as if there were certain "facts one needs to know to solve the snack problem." Then one is led to conclude like Dennett that the frame problem is everybody's problem. But it is Dennett's cognitivist assumptions, not the nature of intelligence, that makes what he calls the frame problem seem intractable.

Since both folk wisdom and 2,000 years of philosophy concur that having a skill is having a capacity to use one's knowledge to reason out solutions to problems, we can defend an alternative perspective only by offering a detailed alternative description of the acquisition and activation of skills. One must be prepared to abandon the traditional view that a beginner starts with specific examples and, as he becomes more proficient, abstracts and interiorizes more and more sophisticated features and rules, and so becomes better and better at solving problems in his skill domain. It might turn out that skill acquisition moves in just the opposite direction: from abstract rules to particular cases, and that figuring things out drops out altogether. Once one looks into the way human beings acquire and use skills one may be less inclined to think of our commonsense capacities as cognitive performances at all. Then the task of eliciting and encoding the supposed context-free facts and rules underlying our knowledge of commonsense physics, human interaction, etc., and the further task of bringing this knowledge to bear when and only when it is relevant, may begin to look less like an occasion for "better models" and "further research" and more like a deep philosophical dead end.

We all have many areas in which are experts so let us look and see how adults learn and use skills:

Stage 1. Novice. Normally, the instruction process begins with the instructor decomposing the task environment into context-free features which the beginner can recognize without benefit of experience. The beginner is then given rules for determining actions on the basis of these features, like a computer following a program. The beginning student wants to do a good job, but lacking any coherent sense of the overall task, he judges his performance mainly by how well he follows his learned rules. After he has acquired more than just a few rules, so much concentration is required during the exercise of his skill that his capacity to talk or listen to advice is severely limited.

For purposes of illustration, and to show the generalities of the model, we shall consider two diverse types of skill: a bodily or motor skill and an intellectual skill. The student automobile driver learns to recognize such interpretation-free features as speed (indicated by his speedometer) and distance (as estimated by a previously acquired skill). Safe following distances are defined in terms of speed; conditions that allow safe entry into traffic are defined in terms of speed and distance of oncoming traffic; timing of shifts of gear is specified in terms of speed, etc. These rules ignore context. They do not refer to traffic density or anticipated stops.

The novice chess player learns a numerical value for each type of piece regardless of its position, and the rule: "always exchange if the total value of pieces captured exceeds the value of pieces lost." He also learns, among other rules, that when no advantageous exchanges can be found center control should be sought, and he is given a rule defining center squares and one for calculating extent of control. Most beginners are notoriously slow players, as they attempt to remember all these rules and their priorities.

Stage 2. Advanced beginner. As the novice gains experience actually coping with real situations, he begins to note, or an instructor points out, perspicuous examples of meaningful additional components of the situation. After seeing a sufficient number of examples, the student learns to recognize them. Instructional maxims now can refer to these new *situational aspects* recognized on the basis of experience, as well as to the objectivity defined *nonsituational features* recognizable by the novice. The advanced beginner confronts his environment, seeks out features and aspects, and determines his actions by applying rules. He shares the novice's minimal concern with quality of performance, instead focusing on quality of rule following. The advanced beginner's performance, while improved, remains slow, uncoordinated, and laborious.

The advanced beginner driver uses (situational) engine sounds as well as (nonsituational) speed in his gear-shifting rules, and observes demeanor as well as position and velocity to anticipate behavior of pedestrians or other drivers. He learns to distinguish the behavior of the distracted or drunken driver from that of the impatient but alert one. No number of words can serve the function of a few choice examples in learning this distinction. Engine sounds cannot be adequately captured by words, and no list of objective facts about a particular pedestrian enables one to predict his behavior in the crosswalk as well as can the driver who has observed many pedetrians crossing streets under a variety of conditions.

With experience, the chess beginner learns to recognize overextended positions. Similarly, he begins to recognize such situational aspects of positions as a weakened king's side or a strong pawn structure despite the lack of precise and universally valid definitional rules.

Stage 3. Competence. With increasing experience, the number of features and aspects to be taken account of becomes overwhelming. To cope with this information explosion, the performer learns, or is taught, to adopt a hierarchical view of decision making. By first choosing a plan, goal, or perspective which organizes the situation and by then examining only the small set of features and aspects that he has learned are the most important given that plan, the performer can simplify and improve his performance.

Choosing a plan, goal, or perspective is no simple matter for the competent performer. It is not an objective procedure, like the feature recognition of the novice. Nor is the choice avoidable. While the advanced beginner can get along without recognizing and using a particular situational aspect until a sufficient number of examples makes identification easy and sure, to perform competently *requires* choosing an organizing goal or perspective. Furthermore, the choice of perspective crucially affects behavior in a way that one particular aspect rarely does.

This combination of necessity and uncertainty introduces an important new type of relationship between the performer and his environment. The novice and the advanced beginner applying rules and maxims feel little or no responsibility for the outcome of their acts. If they have made no mistakes, an unfortunate outcome is viewed as the result of inadequately specified elements or rules. The competent performer, on the other hand, after wrestling with the question of a choice of perspective or goal, feels responsible for, and thus emotionally involved in, the result of his choice. An outcome that is clearly successful is deeply satisfying and leaves a vivid memory of the situation encountered as seen from the goal or perspective finally chosen. Disasters, likewise, are not easily forgotten.

Remembered whole situations differ in one important respect from remembered aspects. The mental image of an aspect is flat in the sense that no parts stand out as salient. A whole situation, on the other hand, since it is the result of a chosen plan or perspective, has a "three-dimensional" quality. Certain elements stand out as more or less important with respect to the plan, while other irrelevant elements are forgotten. Moreover, the competent performer, gripped by the situation that his decision has produced, experiences and therefore remembers the situation not only in terms of foreground and background elements but also in terms of senses of opportunity, risk, expectation, threat, etc. These gripping, holistic memories cannot guide the behavior of the competent performer since he fails to make contact with them when he reflects on problematic situations as a detached observer, and holds to a view of himself as a computer following better and better rules. As we shall soon see, however, if he does let these memories take over, they become the basis of the competent performer's next advance in skill.[1]

A competent driver beginning a trip decides, perhaps, that he is in a hurry. He then selects a route with attention to distance and time, ignores scenic beauty, and as he drives, he chooses his maneuvers with little concern for passenger comfort or for courtesy. He follows more closely than normal, enters traffic more daringly, occasionally violates a law. He feels elated when decisions work out and no police car appears, and is shaken by near accidents and traffic tickets.

A class-A chess player, here categorized as competent, may decide after studying a position that his opponent has weakened his king's defenses so that an attack against the king is a viable goal. If the attack is chosen, features involving weaknesses in his own position created by his attack are ignored as are losses of pieces inessential to the attack. Removal of pieces defending the enemy king becomes salient. Successful plans induce euphoria and mistakes are felt in the pit of the stomach.

In both of these cases, we find a common pattern: detached planning, conscious assessment of elements that are salient with respect to the plan, and analytical, rule-guided choice of action, followed by an emotionally involved experience of the outcome.

Stage 4. Proficiency. Up to this point, the learner of a new skill, to the extent that he has made choices at all rather than merely following rules, has made conscious choices of both goals and actions after reflecting upon various alternatives. As Dennett's discussion of turkey sandwich-making illustrates, this Hamlet model of decision making—the detached, deliberative, and sometimes agonizing selection among alternatives—is taken for granted in the philosophy of action and the psychology of choice. While this type of carefully thought-out behavior certainly sometimes occurs, frequently for learners of new skills and occasionally for even the most skillful, an unbiased examination of our everyday behavior shows it to be the exception rather than the rule.

---

[1] Among philosophers, only Maurice Merleau-Ponty (1983) seems to have a similar appreciation of the role of holistic memories of typical cases in acquiring a skill. "[A]t the decisive moment of learning, a 'now' stands out from the series of 'nows', acquires a particular value and summarizes the groupings which have preceded it as it engages and anticipates the future of the behavior; this 'now' transforms the singular situation of the experience into a typical situation and the effective reaction into a skill" (p. 125).

Considerable experience at the level of competency sets the stage for yet further skill enhancement. Having experienced many situations, chosen plans in each, and having obtained vivid, involved demonstrations of the adequacy or inadequacy of his plans, the performer "notices" or "is struck by" a certain plan, goal or perspective.

According to our account, the proficient performer sees directly what is relevant in his current situation because the current situation calls up a similar experience from the past, already gestalted in terms of issues.[2] But this at first glance seems very mysterious. The current state of affairs is not given in terms of issues until it is seen in terms of a past situation. So how does the brain detect the similarity of a current *meaningless* state of affairs encountered in the real world, not yet seen in terms of salience, to a stored *meaningful* situation already organized in terms of what is important?

If we stood outside the world and represented states of affairs as meaningful objects, situational similarity recognition would be mysterious, indeed. However, we are generally already in a meaningful situation. Except perhaps when awakening in the morning, we do not normally come upon situations in a void. And even when we first awaken we somehow automatically see the situation as similar to a paradigmatic wake-up situation created by prior experiences and stored in memory, causing us, for example, to see as salient certain aspects of the situation related to washing and dressing. From then on throughout the day we gradually move from situation to situation always entering a new one from the perspective of the old.

Since the proficient performer comes into a situation with saliences determined by immediately preceeding events and interpretations, and since he has experienced similar situations seen from a similar perspective in the past, these memories trigger plans similar to those that worked in the past and anticipations of events similar to those that followed in the past. That is, he sees the new situation as similar to a situation which typically follows the one he is in. The new situation may be only a slight variation on the old one, or quite different, depending on events.

When salient aspects change their character—for example, if a smiling expression changes to a smug one—the current situation may not be as similar to the current guiding paradigmatic solution as to some other paradigmatic situation which has roughly the same salient aspects but matches better. This new situation then becomes guiding. Certain aspects of the new paradigmatic situation that now guides behavior will have more or less salience than they did in the old one, and other aspects that were of no significance in the old guiding paradigm may now acquire some importance. Thus the relevance of aspects gradually evolves. No detached choice of deliberation is involved in this evolutionary process.

---

[2] We shall explain below how this associated situation can be called up holistically, i.e., without recourse to symbolic descriptions and rules defining similarity.

Since, however, there are generally far fewer "ways of seeing" than "ways of acting," after understanding without conscious effort what is going on, the proficient performer will still have to think about what to do. During this thinking, elements that present themselves as salient are assessed and combined by rule to produce decisions about how best to manipulate the environment.

On the basis of prior experience, a proficient driver approaching a curve on a rainy day may sense that he is traveling too fast. He then consciously decides whether to apply the brakes, remove his foot from the accelerator, or merely to reduce pressure.

The proficient chess player, who is classed a master, can recognize a large repertoire of types of positions. Recognizing almost immediately and without conscious effort the sense of a position, he sets about calculating the move that best achieves his goal. He may, for example, know that he should attack, but he must deliberate about how best to do so.

Stage 5. Expertise. The proficient performer, immersed in the world of his skillful activity, *sees* what needs to be done, but *decides* how to do it. For the expert, not only situational understandings spring to mind, but also associated appropriate actions. The expert performer, except of course during moments of breakdown, understands, acts, and learns from results without any conscious awareness of the process. What transparently *must* be done *is* done. We usually do not make conscious (or, as far as anyone can tell, unconscious) decisions when we talk, ride a bicycle, drive, make turkey sandwiches, or carry on most social activities. *When things are going well experts do not solve problems or make inferences or figure out anything at all; they simply do what normally works and it normally works.*

We have seen that experience-based, holistic, similarity recognition produces the deep situational understanding of the proficient performer. No new insight is needed to explain the mental processes of the expert. With enough experience with a variety of situations, all seen from the same perspective or with the same goal in mind, but requiring different tactical decisions, the mind of the proficient performer seems gradually to decompose this class of situations into subclasses, each member of which shares not only the same goal or perspective, but also the same decision, action, or tactic. At this point, a situation, when seen as similar to members of this class, is not only thereby understood but simultaneously the associated decision, action, or tactic presents itself.

The number of classes of recognizable situations, built up on the basis of experience, must be immense. It has been estimated that a master chess player can distinguish roughly 50,000 types of positions. Automobile driving probably involves a similar number of typical situations. We doubtless store far more typical situations in our memories than words in our vocabularies. Consequently these reference situations, unlike the situational elements learned by the advanced beginner, bear no names and, in fact, defy complete verbal description.

The expert chess player, classed as an international master or as a grand master, in most situations experiences a compelling sense of the issue and the best move. Excellent chess players can play at the rate of 5–10 seconds a move and even faster without any serious degradation in performance. At this speed they must depend almost entirely on intuition and hardly at all on analysis and comparison of alternatives. We recently performed an experiment in which an international master, Julio Kaplan, was required rapidly to add numbers presented to him audibly at the rate of about 1 number per second while at the same time playing 5-second-a-move chess against a slightly weaker, but master-level, player. Even with his analytical mind completely occupied by adding numbers, Kaplan more than held his own against the master in a series of games. Deprived of the time necessary to see problems or construct plans, Kaplan still produced fluid and coordinated play.

Kaplan's performance seems somewhat less amazing when one realizes that a chess position is as meaningful, interesting, and important to a professional chess player as a face in a receiving line is to a professional politician. Almost anyone can add numbers and simultaneously recognize and respond to faces, even though the face will never exactly match the same face seen previously, and politicians can recognize thousands of faces, just as Julio Kaplan can recognize thousands of chess positions as similar to ones previously encountered.

It seems that a beginner solves problems by making inferences using rules and facts just like a heuristically programmed computer, but that with talent and a great deal of involved experience the beginner develops into an expert who intuitively sees what to do. Of course, a description of skilled behavior can never be taken as conclusive evidence as to what is going on in the mind or in the brain. It is always possible that what is going on is some unconscious process using more and more sophisticated rules. The cognitive scientist might well argue that in spite of appearances the mind and brain *must* be making millions of rapid and accurate inferences like a computer. After all the brain is not "wonder tissue," as Dennett (1984) once accused us of holding, and how else could it work?

But there *are* other models for what might be going on in the hardware. The capacity of experts almost instantaneously and effortlessly to see the present situation as similar to one of tens of thousands of paradigmatic situations suggests that the brain does not work like a heuristically programmed digital computer applying rules to bits of information. Rather it suggests, as some neuropsychologists already believe, that the brain, at times at least, works holographically, superimposing the records of whole situations and measuring their similarity. Dr. Karl Pribram, a Stanford neuropsychologist who has spent the last decade studying holographic memory, explicitly notes the implication of this sort of process for expertise. When asked in an interview (Goleman, 1979) whether holograms would allow a person to make decisions spontaneously in very complex environments, he replied, "Decisions fall out as the holographic correlations are performed. One doesn't have to think things through. . . a step at a time. One takes the whole constellation of a situation, correlates it, and out of that correlation emerges the correct response" (p. 80).

Holographic-like distributed associative memory systems have actually been simulated on digital computers. When used to realize a distributed associative memory, computers no longer use symbols to represent features of the world and computations to represent relationships among these symbols as in traditional AI. Instead, the computer simulates a holistic system (Hinton & Anderson, 1981). One of several such approaches is, indeed, based on the mathematical description of holography. In this system, an input "scene" and its associated output is converted to a distributed representation by a mathematical transformation called a convolution. The convolution produces something akin to the interference pattern stored on a negative in optical holography in that no one element of the convolution corresponds to an element of the input or output, but the input-output pair is distributed throughout all of the elements of the convolution. The input-output convolution is combined with distributed representations of all previously learned associated pairs already in memory so that all share the same computing elements. This memory trace has several remarkable brainlike properties. If an input "scene" which is one member of an associated input-output pair is combined with the trace using a mathematical formula called a correlation, the other member of the associated pair is produced. This happens even if the input "scene" is only a large part of the original whole "scene," or is similar but not identical with the original "scene." A "scene" can be anything representable as a string of digits. At one extreme, the most common, the scene is a digitized representation of a picture with the digits representing the light intensity at various points. Or, at the other extreme, if one chooses to see the world in terms of a typical AI description, it can be a representation of features that are present and absent in a situation. But even in this latter case, features are not stored as lists in distinct locations or processed according to recognizable rules (For more details, see Hinton & Anderson, 1981, or Eich, 1982, which contains an extensive set of references.)

If we contrast skill representations and knowledge representations, we can appreciate the frame problem. Skilled human beings have, in the areas of their expertise, an understanding based on past experience which is

of course, as one adds more and more subscripts, each with its preselected relevant features and its own subscripts, the complexity of the whole account rapidly increases. It is purely an act of faith for AI researchers like Schank that such a model can capture human restaurant behavior before the formalism becomes hopelessly complicated. The simple version is easily manageable. But that is no evidence it is a successful step toward human understanding.

Even if one shares Schank's faith that scripts can eventually capture the stereotypical side of restaurant behavior, with the proliferation of frames comes the question: How does one move from one frame to another? To keep to the restaurant example, suppose in the "seeing someone you know" frame the conversation with that person gives you new information. The friend might tell you that an old friend is in town for only one more hour, or that he just saw your small child running down the street unescorted, or that the service just made him sick, or that a company in whose stock you hold a short position is about to become the object of a takeover, or that someone you are trying to avoid is eating in the next room, and so on. Each bit of news would set you off in a different direction. From the frame point of view the next frame would be either: leaving as soon as possible, running out of the restaurant, ordering only cooked food, telephoning your broker, or asking for a table on the terrace. In order to give the computer the capacity to cope with this kind of change, the frame approach would have to include rules for how to select a next frame. It seems incredible that one could write, and that we actually use, such rules, and indeed no one has ever tried to provide them.

Even if the problems of frame proliferation and frame change could be solved, it is a huge leap to Schank's (1984) claim that "the restaurant script contains all the information necessary to understand the enormous variability of what can occur in a restaurant" (p. 177). Schank doesn't even try to deal with the question of motivation. Yet, to make sense of restaurant behavior one not only has to understand *what* people typically do in eating establishments, but *why* they do it. Thus, even if he could manage to list all that was *possibly* relevant in typical restaurant going, we would be left with no understanding of what at any point in time was *actually* relevant for the person involved.

Going to a restaurant is like most everyday situations. We face a continually branching web of possible situations, each of which is sized up in terms of some issue. Only then do the relevant facts show up as salient. For example, if you go out to eat in Berkeley, you have a choice between the smoking and nonsmoking section. What might become relevant here includes, among other factors, whether a table is free in the section one prefers, and if not, what stage of their meals the current customers are in. Moreover, which of these factors actually becomes important to you de-

pends on how hungry you are, how rushed, and how comfortable the wait-
ing area, and many other things. As time passes, all such factors continually
change. One's concerns also change and with them one's sense of which
factors are relevant. After you move to a table, you consider the question
of who sits where, which introduces new factors such as comfort, view,
sex, and age—all of which have no fixed relevance but whose importance
again depends on your perspective. And when you order, you do not sum-
mon up a fixed frame in which everything relevant has been determined
once and for all. Some *possible* concerns are: What is fresh, how long does
it take to prepare, how much does it cost, what did you eat earlier that day
and expect to eat later that day, what dietary principles do you follow and
how strictly. This open-ended list sets out what *might* be important to
you, but only your sense of things, gained perhaps by talking to the waiter
and your past experiences of restaurant going, determines what is actually
relevant as you decide what to eat.

To bring out the proper place and limits of the frame approach it helps
to contrast a dynamical, continuously changing activity such as restaurant-
going with a situation in which static, discrete scripts might actually capture human capacities. Such a situation would, of course, have to be completely defined by a discrete and limited set of features that would permit
only a discrete and limited set of responses. Moreover, motivation would
play no part because at each stage in the script there would be only one
right thing to do. Thus no expertise would be required or acquired since
there would be no question of seeing the issue in the current situation or of
passing from issue to issue as events unfolded.

Placing a phone call may well constitute such a situation. It is so simple that no strategy is needed; there is one right way to do things. Fodor
(1983, pp. 113–114) has trouble making the frame problem seem serious—
and so eventually switches to a much more difficult problem—precisely
because he first tries this easily programmed case. In the phone case, the
frame problem can be finessed simply by using a frame that lists all possible
events and the appropriate reaction to each. For example, a super-smart
modem could store some sort of frame for typical phoning situations. Such
a frame would include cases of misdialing, wrong number, changed number, unlisted number, malfunctioning phone, busy, no answer, poor connection, crossed lines, cut off, answering machine, successful connection,
etc. With each could be paired an appropriate response or set of responses.
Eventualities not relevant to making a phone call need not be considered
at all. True, when placing a call the phone ceases to be free to outside calls;
the dial tone cuts off and gets replaced by beeps; something happens in a
computer at the central exchange; and so forth. But these are not relevant
to making an ordinary phone call. Such possibilities might be listed in the
frame of a robot programmed for phone repair, but they are not changes a
person has to check out each time he or she dials a call.

Being electronic devices, phones lend themselves to modular designs—that's what makes a phone-repair robot, or at least a phone-fault-diagnosis program, a possibility. But a mechanical device even as simple as an automobile has a high number of interacting components, connected together in ways that produce complex and synergistic patterns of breakdown, with multiple and poorly delimited submodules each capable of occupying a continuum of states between proper and improper functioning. Accordingly, no set of frames can capture the knowledge necessary for expert diagnosis. Indeed, to the extent that any electronic device has these properties, it too will resist automated diagnosis.

The shifting relevance of aspects of ordinary changing situations would certainly be grounds for despair in AI and Cognitive Science were it not for the fact that human beings seem to get along fine in a changing world. Cognitivists assume that this shows that human beings must somehow be able to update their formal representations and thus the frame problem must be soluble. We, however, have argued that it can more plausibly be read as showing that human, skillful know-how is not represented as a mass of facts organized in frames and scripts specifying in a step-wise sequence which facts must be taken account of as the state of affairs evolves. Rather, as we saw when describing proficient performers, memories of past experience with situations similar to the present one, plus the ability to recognize this similarity without recourse to descriptions and rules, seems sufficient to account for the ability to cope with change. The important point is that we human beings proceed from the past into the future with our past experience always going before us organizing the way the next event shows up for use. Thus we do not need to deal with real-world situations by listing in advance all possibly relevant features plus rules for determining under what circumstances each feature may become actually relevant, and rules for when these rules are relevant, etc.

The frame problem—the problem of keeping track of all facts affected by all changes—shows the difficulty of substituting the computer's static, discontinuous, flat descriptions for the human capacity to transform past experiences into a continuous perception of changing relevance. Unless AI scientists can produce programs in which representations of past experiences encoded in terms of salience can directly affect the way current situations show up, they will be stuck with some version of the frame problem and be unable to get their computers to cope with change. The outlook is grim for AI, however, since the way human beings use past experience to cope with the future seems to require two capacities unavailable to heuristically programmed digital computers: pictorial representation and direct recognition of similarity.

Unfortunately for AI, memories which reflect salience are like images, but computers cannot directly use images or any picture-like representations of objects and situations. They can only make inferences from *descrip-*

tions. Likewise, computers cannot deal with similarity except by analyzing it into a list of identical features. Douglas Lenat (1984) points out, in a way quite in line with the views presented in this paper, that what computers lack is the ability to learn from experience and to apply what they know by recognizing the similarity of past experience to the present situation. As he sees it, this problem literally throws the computer scientist for a loop:

> On the one hand, computer programs will have to become a lot more knowledgeable before they will be able to reason effectively by analogy. On the other hand, to acquire knowledge in such bulk it would seem that computers must at least be able to "understand" analogy when it is presented to them . . . The problem is thus of the chicken-and-egg sort. (p. 209)

Lenat (1984) acknowledges that no one knows how to program a computer to take account of similarities, to *"reason"* by analogy as he tendentiously puts it, and falls back on the usual "first step" claim plus an empty gesture towards future research:

> A little introspection and an attentive ear are all it takes to realize that people draw on analogy constantly in explaining and understanding concepts and in finding new ones. This source of power is only beginning to be exploited by intelligent software, but it will doubtless be the focus of future research. (p. 209)

As long as the use of images and analogy remain vague promises, heuristically programmed digital computers will not be able to approach the way human beings are able to cope with changing relevance.

We have so far discussed two interrelated problems blocking progress in AI and Cognitive Science: (a) Human-like intelligence requires an understanding of the everyday physical and social world which for cognitivists requires representing a huge number of facts, while for human beings such background understanding seems to take the form of skills rather than explicit knowledge. And (b), for the computer instantiating a formal description, coping with the changing world requires efficiently representing all the relevant facts at a given time, as well as all the ways that what counts as a relevant fact can change—the frame problem. For human beings, however, situations show up with relevance or salience built in, along with anticipations, based on past experience of similar meaningful situations, of how what is relevant will change as the situation develops.

There is a third human capacity which AI researchers have also so far found impossible to duplicate—a person's ability to see the relevance, in a situation with which he or she is already familiar, of certain events which have never before been experienced in this context. For example, if a horse player who bets using his sense of the similarity of the current horse, jockey, weather, etc. to past patterns were to discover that the race-course landscaping was in full flower and that one of the jockeys had hay fever, he might well see the relevance for his bet of these two normally irrelevant and unrelated facts (Dreyfus, 1979). How could common sense be organized so as to allow this ability? Fodor (1983) identifies this problem with the frame problem, and it is, indeed, a problem of changing relevance, but it is much harder than the AI problem of coping with everyday familiar change. It cannot be solved by showing how people see whole changing situations as similar to whole familiar situations from the past.

Data structures of preclassified, commonsense facts dear to AI researchers cannot account for this amazing capacity to see *new* relevance; but our claim that through experience each person has embodied a great deal of commonsense know-how does not help either. Such new facts would not be included in a frame for horse-race betting, but neither would they show up as salient for a skilled human being, even though his past went ahead of him organizing his world. There is a sort of everyday creativity which seems to be equally beyond the grasp of cognitivism and of phenomenology.

REFERENCES

Dreyfus, H. (1979). *What computers can't do*. New York: Harper and Row.

Eich, J.M. (1982). A composite holographic associative recall memory. *Psychological Review*, 89(6), 627–661.

Fodor, J. (1983). *The modularity of mind*. Cambridge, MA: MIT Press, A Bradford Book.

Goleman, D. (1979). Holographic memory: An interview with Karl Pribram. *Psycology Today*, 12(9), 80.

Hinton, G., & Anderson, J. (Eds.). (1981). *Parallel models of associative memory*. Hillsdale, NJ: Erlbaum.

Lenat, D. (1984). Computer software for intelligent systems. *Scientific American*, 251, 204–213.

Merleau-Ponty, M. (1983). *The structure of behavior*. Pittsburgh, PA: Duquesne University Press.

Minsky, M. (1975). A framework for representing knowledge. In P.H. Winston (Ed.), *The psychology of computer vision*. New York: McGraw-Hill.

Schank, R.C. (1975). The primitive acts of conceptual dependency. *Theoretical issues in natural language processing*. Cambridge, MA:

Schank, R.C., & Childers, P.G. (1984). *The cognitive computer*. Reading, MA: Addison-Wesley.

CHAPTER 6

We've Been Framed:
Or, Why AI Is Innocent of
the Frame Problem

Drew McDermott

Yale University

Home for Christmas, both my wife and I decided to use the laundry room at the same time. I was soaking a tablecloth in the sink. She was using the washing machine. We both knew that Mom's washing machine discharged into the sink, so we should have been able to infer that stopping it up would cause a deluge. After the deluge, in fact, we diagnosed the cause instantly.

This is an example of failing to make an "obviously" useful inference. It is widely believed that there is a special problem of getting machines to do as well as people in making all the useful inferences in a situation without any of the useless ones. This is often called the "frame problem." In this paper, I will argue that:

1. There is no one problem here; and hence no solution is possible or necessary.

Thanks to Eugene Charniak and Larry Birnbaum for helping to clarify arguments and counterarguments. This work was supported by a grant from the Office of Naval Research, No. N00014-83-K-9281.

2. The interesting problem originally identified by the phrase "frame problem" has been lost in the noise surrounding the vague collection of issues that the phrase has come to denote.

Let's start with Number 2. The original frame problem arose in connection with a proposal of McCarthy (1958; McCarthy and Hayes, 1969) for representing temporally conditioned facts. His idea was (in essence, but altering the notation) to represent a fact like "Fred is in the kitchen" by making explicit the *situation* referred to, thus:

True_in(situation409, in(Fred, kitchen))

so that in(Fred,kitchen) is a term denoting a *fact*, true in some situations and not in others.

Events were to be represented as transitions between situations. The term result(*situation, event*) denoted a new situation resulting from the given *event* occurring in *situation*. The "physics" of the world was specified by axioms like

$$\forall (x,y,s)(\text{True\_in}(s,\text{animate}(x)) \supset \text{True\_in}(\text{result}(s,\text{go}(x,y)),\text{in}(x,y)))$$

that is, "If an object is animate, it will be in a location it goes to."

Unfortunately, in this formalism it is necessary to provide a large number of "frame axioms," which state that a fact remains unchanged by events of most kinds. For instance, going from place to place leaves one's color unchanged:

$$\forall (x,y,c,s)(\text{True\_in}(s,\text{color}(x,c)) \supset \text{True\_in}(\text{result}(s,\text{go}(x,y)),\text{color}(x,c)))$$

Since most events leave most facts untouched, most axioms in the system will be of this tedious kind. Most steps of a proof about time will be aimed at proving that something is still true in a given situation by stringing together such axioms.

There are several reasons why this is an interesting technical problem for artificial intelligence. I will discuss these reasons shortly. However, when philosophers discuss this problem, they focus on an entirely different set of issues. I hope that what follows will make it clear why this set is ultimately of less interest.

The frame problem manifests itself in three ways: logical, computational, and "metaphysical." The logical aspect (the one McCarthy has focused on since he first described the frame problem) is to leave the essential theory intact, but get rid of the excess tonnage of frame axioms. The solution is to use nonmonotonic logic (Sandewall, 1972; McCarthy, 1980) to condense all the frame axioms into one:

> "If a fact is true in a situation, and it cannot be proven that it is untrue in the situation resulting from an event, then it is still true."

or something like that. I will not dwell on this, because I believe that solving the logical frame problem for the original situation calculus is of little importance. It raises many fascinating issues in nonmonotonic logic, and is thereby a useful environment for studying such logics, but it neglects the other, more interesting, aspects.

The computational aspect of the problem is to infer efficiently that a fact is still true in a situation. Regardless of the solution to the logical problem as I described it, it is still the case that the length of a proof that a fact remains true through a sequence of events is proportional to the number of events. The time required to find the proof may be much larger.

Fortunately, this problem is not nearly as bad as it sounds. No one has attempted to use a theorem prover to do problem solving since Cordell Green's (1969) work in the 'sixties. In all systems since then, starting with STRIPS (Fikes and Nilsson, 1971), programs have used what Haugeland calls the "sleeping dog" strategy. They keep track of each situation as a separate database. To reason about result(s, e), they compute all the effects of e in situation s, make those changes, and leave the rest of s (the "sleeping dogs") alone. Now to find if something is true in a given situation, the program need check only the database describing that situation. (The tricky part technically is to copy almost all of a database without touching any of its contents; see McDermott, 1983.)

This is the first opportunity for philosophers to misunderstand. It is of course quite possible for a program to make a mistake in updating a situation description. But it is just as possible for humans to make a mistake, as my story at the beginning of the paper illustrates.

Before pursuing that point, let me describe the metaphysical aspect of the frame problem. The situation calculus is inadequate to talk about most things that go on in nature. The washing machine scenario is a good example. The result of pushing the "start" button on the machine starts processes in motion that cannot be described as a set of facts about the state result(. . . ,pushbutton(. . .)). These processes exist over a continuum of states, during which other things are happening.

Let us take a particularly simple example. I introduced the term go (*agent, location*) above to denote an event. I could also have a term eat (*agent, food*). What is the relation between these two situations?

result(situation563, go(Fred, living_room))
result(situation563, eat(Fred, ham_sandwich303))?

Are they alternatives, as McCarthy usually implies? That would limit Fred to doing one or the other. If we allow them both to exist in the same universe, then we can start to ask awkward questions like, Which comes first? Even worse, our frame axioms begin to be false. A frame axiom to the effect that "Your location after eating a ham sandwich is the same as before" is falsified by ambulatory munchers.

For reasons like these, the past few years have seen several attempts to revise temporal ontology and reasoning patterns. The ontological work (Allen, 1984; Hayes, 1985; McDermott, 1982) talks in terms of temporal intervals over which many things happen at once. The computational work (Dean, 1984; Forbus, 1984; Kuipers, 1984; Simmons, 1984; Vere, 1983) presents programs that reason about continuous processes, deadlines, and other things. I won't go into this stuff in detail, but two remarks are relevant here. First, the frame problem appears again, but not as what's true in the next situation given that it was true in the previous situation, because in a continuous world there is no "next" situation. Instead, it appears as the problem of whether you can infer that something is still true given what you know about what has happened since it became true.

Second, it is still the case, as it has been since 1970, that *no working AI program has ever been bothered at all by the frame problem.* The "sleeping dog" approach outlined above carries over nicely to the newer frameworks. If you look at what AI researchers are actually concerned about in the time domain, you will find a quite different set of issues: What is the proper level of analysis for a mechanism? How can conclusions be drawn from qualitative descriptions? How can a large time map be stored and accessed efficiently? How do you manage the search through alternative sets of plans?

The original frame problem is, in fact, of interest mainly to a fringe group, those who believe that logical analyses are relevant to building knowledge representations. I count myself in this group, and it is a major embarrassment to us that logic stumbles over such a trivial hurdle as the frame problem. We would dearly love to have a formalism which really was as powerful and perspicuous as McCarthy's situation calculus appeared to be at first.

Now let us turn to the philosophers. For unclear reasons, they have seen a special obstacle to the sleeping dog idea. As I said above, for this approach to work, it must be possible for a program to infer from an event description that certain things are going to change, and to leave other things alone. The perceived obstacle is that an infinite number of changes could be noted. Sometimes we are asked to ponder the infinite number of *potential* changes that might occur, almost all of which must be examined and ruled out.

Stated carefully, the argument is as follows:

> There are *two* subproblems raised by the sleeping dog approach to the frame problem. The first half has been solved (modulo bookkeeping); it is the problem of leaving most things unchanged as time goes by. Let us call this the "inertia problem." Unfortunately, solving it leaves the other half, predicting all the changes due to an event. Since this "prediction problem" is still immense, you have only half a solution, and that's no solution at all.

This argument is an unwarranted raising of the stakes. The original frame problem involved very simple situations, in which it was not difficult to make all the required predictions. At this point, the believers in the frame problem (let us call them "framists") start to make the situation more complicated, arguing that the bounds of what machines can predict are passed along before we reach the bounds of what is predictable at all.

I have never seen a convincing example, all proposals being either too easy for machines or too hard for anyone, including humans. A commonly cited situation in Hayes's (1971) cup-and-saucer problem, in which a pull on a saucer must give rise to a prediction that the cup sitting on it moves as well. It seems incredible to me that a prediction like this is held to be beyond the powers of a simple algorithm.

At this point the example is usually elaborated to include a string tying the cup to an immovable object. And at this point the framist throws up his hands. I don't blame him. No one has the foggiest idea how to reason about nonrigid objects like strings in a realistic way. However, it seems to me that this is the "string problem," which is a subset of the "object motion" problem, which is a subset of the "naive physics" problem. It contributes nothing to the discussion to say it is something called the "frame problem." To say this is to presuppose that the problem is either solved in the human mind, or made moot there by some entirely different way of organizing things. I doubt that either of these is the case, and the evidence seems to be on my side; people (or is it just I?) do indeed make many silly blunders in the course of a given week.

The framists have a comeback to this argument:

> There you go again, compartmentalizing knowledge in unlikely ways. It is wishful thinking to suppose that all the relevant information about one's situation can be filed under convenient categories like the "string frame."

To some extent, I think, this comeback is a misreading of the literature on frames. But this literature is of little importance to the frame problem anyway (its apparent relevance being due to the unfortunate overuse of the word "frame"), so let's try to clear away from the argument any of its dependence on theories of frames (or "stereotypes," or "scripts"). I think the essence of the argument is this:

> When we try to write down an algorithm for predicting what will happen when something is pulled, we are soon overwhelmed by the complexities. It's just impossible.

Well, let's try it. Here is the first draft of an algorithm:

ALGORITHM FOR FIGURING OUT WHAT HAPPENS WHEN AN OBJECT "TUGGEE" IS TUGGED UPON IN DIRECTION D

Examine the surface tuggee is resting on.

> It could be approximately horizontal, could curve downward in the direction of pull, or curve upward.

> If horizontal, then friction will oppose the pull; if down or up, gravity will be a factor.

Find everything connected directly or indirectly to tuggee.

> How can things be connected?
> > An object can be resting on the tuggee
> > It can be pushed by the tuggee (in direction D)
> > It can be pulled
> > It can be rigidly attached (e.g., glued)
>
> Compute the transitive closure of the attachment relation. For instance, if a saucer is being pulled, and a teacup is sitting on it tied to an anvil, then the teacup, string, and anvil are all attached to the saucer.

Figure out what forces oppose the tug. These include frictional forces, gravity, tension in strings.

> Find the "weak links" in the situation (e.g., strings that could break, supported objects that could be left behind).

> If the forces are greater than the weak links, movement will occur. However, a weak link may snap, causing everything connected through it to be left behind. For instance, the cup and anvil may be left behind when the saucer is pulled. If it is not clear what forces win out, report: "Hard to predict."

As I admitted above, there are severe representational problems in actually implementing this algorithm today. But that's not the issue. The issue is whether it leaves out most of the relevant considerations, in an unfixable way. I claim it does not. Undoubtedly there are situations this algorithm can't handle. A large enough jumble of strings and blocks will cause it to give up. But so what? It isn't as if there's a right answer here that the algorithm is overlooking. Any complex system about which only rough, qualitative information is available will behave in unpredictable ways.

The only practical solution to the prediction problem is to select a model of the situation and use it to make inferences. The algorithm I just gave is a model of the cup-and-saucer world. In the washing-machine anecdote, the model specified that an effect of pushing the "on" button of a washing machine was to start a washing process. Any model must omit much of what will actually happen, such as the fate of the drain water or the consumption of electricity. Hence any real inference maker will tend to overlook potentially useful inferences. Occasionally a too-detailed model will be selected, and too many inferences will be made. Obviously there are interesting technical questions about how the right model is selected and how it is cranked to generate results. But there is no interesting question about how to avoid generating an infinite number of irrelevant inferences.

Surely if the frame problem in the framists' sense really existed, someone would be working on it. But I am unaware of anyone in AI who claims to be working on it. In fact, as I said above, even the original frame problem is of interest only to a small group of logicist researchers.

At this point I begin to suspect that when framists say the words "frame problem," they really mean "AI problem." Philosophical exegeses of the problem often take the form of a painful series of examples difficult for any algorithm to handle. Curiously enough, much of AI research takes much the same form. For instance, some research (Brooks, 1982; Lozano-Perez, 1981; Kuipers, 1978; McDermott & Davis, 1984) has been done on robot navigation. It involves finding paths or obstacles between the robot and its target, and plotting routes to conform to them. No one (to my knowledge) has allowed the robot to change vehicles along the way (e.g., walk to the bicycle, bike to the bus stop, take the bus to the river, etc.). Partly this is because there are plenty of interesting problems without thinking about vehicles, but partly it is because it is not obvious how to integrate vehicle choice with the other choices to be made along the way. If you select the vehicle before starting, based on distance, you may miss felicitous options that take advantage of features of the terrain (e.g., a monorail station). If you plot the route in a "vehicle-free" way, hoping to put the vehicles in later, you may find a good path for, say, walking across country, and now know how to improve it using vehicles.

AI researchers are quite familiar with this phenomenon, where the order of choices is crucial, and any order has problems. Even when a program falls back on search techniques, which can recover from bad guesses, the order of guesses can be the difference between a practical search algorithm and a useless one. What's frustrating is that often one's research is carried on under the silent, mocking gaze of the human mind, which performs the task tolerably well without hinting at how hard it is working. Introspection about vehicle selection tells you little except that people often pick the right vehicle.

It seems to be a matter of temperament whether one feels discouraged or challenged by such difficulties. If challenged, one becomes an AI researcher; if discouraged, one suddenly discerns a "frame problem" that explains why the going is so slow. This discovery is not only otiose; it also tends to suggest that people have a unitary ability to focus on the relevant aspects of a situation and ignore the irrelevant aspects.

One is tempted to believe in such an ability when one realizes that vehicles are only part of the problem. What about plotting routes to handle several errands? What about preferring to avoid going out in the rain? What about tollbooths? What if you are moving lots of things at once (e.g., an army through mountainous terrain)? What if you know you need to ask directions along the way? What if night falls before you arrive at your destination?

With all these different dimensions, it *does* begin to seem incredible that there can be an algorithm that takes them all into account. However, it is even more incredible that there is *something else* that can take them all into account. Furthermore, when all these factors become relevant, humans start to overlook some of them, and to make the same sort of blunders the algorithms do.

Sometimes framists conclude by saying that some tasks require special-purpose hardware, and that therefore AI is misguided. Some AI people don't like this kind of conclusion, but others welcome it, so long as it is understood that hardware solutions merely *speed up* algorithms, not obviate them. The mind may well consist of nothing but a large collection of special-purpose boxes; the absurdity is to suppose that it consists of just one "magic" box that "solves the frame problem" or in some other way cuts through all the difficulties.

Anyway, until someone explains to me exactly what the frame problem is, I have only one suggestion to make. Let us adopt the term "inertia problem" for the technical problem of managing temporal systems in which most facts seldom change. This label clearly identifies the problem as nothing but that of getting our representations to handle nonchange as smoothly as we do. The problem of noticing all and only relevant inferences about change will never have, and does not need, a solution.

REFERENCES

Allen, J. (1984). Towards a general theory of action and time. *Artificial Intelligence, 23* (2), 123–154.

Brooks, R. (1982). Solving the find-path problem by good representation of space. In *Proceedings of the American Association for Artificial Intelligence* (pp. 381–386).

Dean, T. (1984). Temporal reasoning with metric constraints. *Proceedings of the Canadian Society for Computational Studies of Intelligence, 84,* 28–32.

Fikes, R., & Nilsson, N.J. (1971). STRIPS: A new approach to the application of theorem proving to problem solving. *Artificial Intelligence, 2,* 189–208.

Forbus, K. (1984). *Qualitative process theory.* Unpublished doctoral dissertation, Massachusetts Institute of Technology.

Green, C.C. (1969). *The application of theorem proving to question-answering systems.* Unpublished doctoral dissertation, Stanford University.

Hayes, P.J. (1971). A logic of actions. In B. Meltzer & D. Michie (Eds.), *Machine Intelligence 6* (pp. 495–520). New York: Wiley.

Hayes, P.J. (1985). Naive physics I: Ontology for liquids. In J. Hobbs & R. Moore (Eds.), *Formal theories of the commonsense world* (pp. 71–107). Norwood, NJ: Ablex.

Kuipers, B. (1978). Modeling spatial knowledge. *Cognitive Science, 2* (2), 129–154.

Kuipers, B. (1984). Commonsense reasoning about causality: Deriving behavior from structure. *Artificial Intelligence, 24* (1), 169–203.

Lozano-Perez, T. (1981). Automatic planning of manipulator transfer movements. *IEEE Transactions on Systems, Man, & Cybernetics, 11* (6), 681–698.

McCarthy, J. (1958). Programs with common sense. *Proceedings of the Symposium on Mechanization of Thought Processes.* (Also in M. Minsky (Ed.) (1968), *Semantic information processing* (pp. 403–418). Cambridge, MA: MIT Press.)

McCarthy, J. (1980). Circumscription: A nonmonotonic inference rule. *Artificial Intelligence, 13* (1,2), 27–40.

McCarthy, J., & Hayes, P. (1969). Some philosophical problems from the standpoint of artificial intelligence. In B. Meltzer & D. Michie (Eds.), *Machine Intelligence 4.* Edinburgh, Scotland: Edinburgh University Press.

McDermott, D. (1982). A temporal logic for reasoning about processes and plans. *Cognitive Science, 6,* 101–155.

McDermott, D. (1983). Contexts and data dependencies: A synthesis. *IEEE Transactions on Pattern Analysis and Machine Intelligence, 5* (3), 237–246.

McDermott, D., & Davis, E. (1984). Planning routes through uncertain territory. *Artificial Intelligence, 22,* 107–156.

Meltzer, B., & Michie, D. (Eds.). (1969). *Machine Intelligence 4.* Edinburgh, Scotland: Edinburgh University Press.

Meltzer, B., & Michie, D. (Eds.). (1971). *Machine Intelligence 6.* New York: Wiley.

Meltzer, B., & Michie, D. (Eds.). (1972). *Machine Intelligence 7*. New York: Wiley.

Minsky, M. (Ed.). (1968). *Semantic information processing*. Cambridge, MA: MIT Press.

Sandewall, E. (1972). An approach to the frame problem and its implementation. In B. Meltzer & D. Michie (Eds.), *Machine Intelligence 7* (pp. 195–204). Edinburgh, Scotland: Edinburgh University Press.

Simmons, R. (1983). The use of qualitative and quantitative simulations. *Proceedings of the American Association for Artificial Intelligence* (pp. 364–368).

Vere, S. (1983). Planning in time: Windows and durations for activities and goals. *IEEE Transactions on Pattern Analysis and Machine Intelligence, 5*(3), 246–267.

CHAPTER 7

What the Frame Problem Is and Isn't

Patrick J. Hayes

University of Rochester

The term "frame problem" is due to John McCarthy, and was introduced in McCarthy and Hayes (1969). It is generally used within the AI field in something close to its original meaning. Others, however, especially philosophers, sometimes interpret the term in different ways; for examples, see the papers in this volume by Dennet, Fodor, and Haugeland. In this short paper I will try to state clearly and informally what the frame problem is, distinguish it from other problems with which it is often confused, briefly survey the currently available partial solutions to it, and respond to some of the sillier misunderstandings.

One might argue that what a problem is *called* is of no real or lasting consequence, but that what matters is what the problems are, and how hard they are to solve. Whereas I have much sympathy with this point of view, it is important to get the names right when one hopes to communicate with others, or misunderstandings are liable to occur. Throughout this paper, to emphasize, the term "frame problem" will be used in its original sense, which is not the way it is used in several other papers in this book, including the introduction.

WHAT THE FRAME PROBLEM IS

The frame problem arises in the following context. One is trying to model cognition by a process of deduction in a suitable logical theory. The task is to write down axioms in, say, first-order logic, which state what it is that a simple "thinker" would have in its mind, in such a way that the conclusions which a rational creature would draw, follow fairly straightforwardly from them. The aim is that, as nearly as possible, obvious conclusions have short derivations.[1] So, how is this theory to be built? What vocabulary does it use? What ontology underlies it? This is called the Problem of Representation in AI, and has been recognized as the central area since the field's inception a quarter of a century ago. This is not the frame problem.

Once one has developed some suitable representation of the world about which the reasoner is expected to reason, one needs also to arrange that the system performs deductions which are appropriate for its assigned tasks and doesn't get lost in clouds of valid but irrelevant conclusions. (It is fairly easy to arrange that it doesn't generate invalid conclusions.) This is variously called the theorem-proving problem, or the control problem, or the search problem, in AI. This is not the frame problem either.[2]

The frame problem arises when the reasoner is thinking about a changing, dynamic world, one with actions and events in it. Much AI work isn't concerned with such domains, but restricts itself to thinking about things which don't change, or change in very carefully restricted and predictable ways. Game-playing programs, most "expert systems," and such things as designer's assistants and many so-called natural-language "comprehension" systems are thus protected from the intricacies of dynamic worlds, so they are never concerned about the frame problem: It simply doesn't arise in their reasonings. It only becomes an annoyance when one tries to describe a world of the sort that people, animals, and robots inhabit, in which things move around, in which the relations and properties which one seems to need in the representation are labile, alterable by actions and events; for example, a world in which things move from place to place.

How can such a world be described? AI hackers and philosophical logicians converged some time ago on the same general idea. One introduces states or time-instants or situations or temporally possible worlds or world-states (or whatever: I will use the terms interchangeably) into the ontology of the theory and uses them as temporal indices, as a way of distinguishing what is true at one time from what is true at another. Any relations, prop-

---

[1] The use of logic as a representational language in this way has been extremely controversial within the AI field, and some have strongly urged that other languages or notations are more suitable. There seems now to be a fairly wide consensus that most of these can be seen as variations or enrichments of first-order logic, or occasionally higher order logic, however.

[2] Of course, the control problem does not follow on the heels of the representation problem in quite this neat a way in practice. The choice of representation is often governed by computational issues, for example, and many search and control questions are studied in the abstract, divorced from the details of any particular representational language. This brief introduction slurs over volumes of complication and controversy. Nevertheless, it is essentially correct; enough for our purposes here, anyway.

erties, or functions whose value is liable to change with time are treated as being relations between their static values and these time-instants, so that one would have the concept of where a thing is located *at a certain instant,* or what the temperature is *at a certain instant,* and so on.[3] Now, events or actions or changes are thought of as functions from instants to instants, or perhaps relations between instants, and this enables one to state the effects of actions by describing what will be true of the state which the action produces: So, an (oversimplified) axiom about movement might say something like

> IF the agent is in room *r* in state *s,*
>   AND IF the door *d* from *r* to *r1* is open in state *s,*
>   THEN the agent is in *r1* in state *gothru(d,s)*

In this way, with some rather more intricate axioms, one can make axiom sets, inferences from which do indeed seem to model reasonably well what might be called rational reasoning about courses of action in simple worlds.

But here, at last, is the frame problem. With axioms like the above, it is possible to infer what the immediate consequences of actions are. But what about the immediate non-consequences? When I go through a door, my position changes. But the color of my hair, and the positions of the cars in the streets, and the place my granny is sitting, don't change. In fact, most of the world carries on in just the same way that it did before, or would have done if I hadn't gone into room r1. But since many of these things CAN change, they are described in our vocabulary as being relative to the time-instant, so we cannot directly infer, as a matter of logic, that they are true in state *gothru(d,s)* just because they were in state *s:* This needs to be stated somehow in our axioms. In this ontology, whenever something MIGHT change from one moment to another, we have to find some way of stating that it DOESN'T change whenever ANYTHING changes. And this seems silly, since almost all changes in fact change very little of the world. One feels that there should be some economical and principled way of succinctly saying what changes an action makes, without having to explicitly list all the things it doesn't change as well; yet there doesn't seem to be any other way to do it. *That* is the frame problem. If there are 100 actions, and 500 labile properties and relations, then we might need 50,000 of these silly "frame axioms," stating that if, for example, my hair color is *c* in state *s,* then it's also *c* in state *gothru(d,s),* and in state *pickup(object,s), and state*

---

[3] One can think of this in several different ways. Instants can be thought of as being possible worlds, so that they *contain* objects and relations for a moment; or as mere identifiers, so that the relations are *between* them and the objects, which are now thought of as lasting for some time. Or, one can transcribe the whole theory in the way preferred by McDermott, where there is a single relation TRUE-AT holding between whole propositions and the time-instants. Formally, these are all equivalent.

drive(start,finish,s), *etc.*, but not in state *dyehair(c1,s)*, which is why it has to be state relative.

Another way of stating the problem is this: Imagine one has a large number of facts about a particular state, as it were, a snapshot of a moving universe, and a description of an action—recall, this is to be thought of as a function from states to states—which is sufficient to enable you to infer what will be true at the new time just after the action. How big a description will you need? The naive intuition is that the description of the action could be fairly small, something like the axiom about rooms and doors above. But—and this is the frame problem—it seems that it will in fact have to be as big as the description of the time-instant itself, specifying for *every* changeable fact whether or not it changes that fact. This would perhaps be acceptable if indeed actions did produce widespread changes in the world, if there were great complexity to be decribed. But in fact they don't, and almost all of this action description consists of a monotonous litany of reassurance that this action doesn't change this or that or the other. And this is unacceptable, for many reasons.[4] The problem is to find a more principled, compact, and sensible way to state or infer these platitudes, or somehow avoid the need to infer them at all.

The frame problem is sometimes dismissed as being a narrow, technical problem of little philosophical interest, the sort of glitch that the hackers will sort out by themselves. I think this is a mistake. For one thing, a "narrow technical problem" which is this immediate, this central, this devastating, and this resistant to solution is worthy of some respect. For another, the ontological framework in which it arises is exactly that which provides the foundation for much of modern philosophical logic, which should give some slight cause for concern. But in any case, the problem identifies an issue of some philosophical interest in its own right: what ordinariness means.

Imagine explaining the monkey-and-bananas problem to someone. A monkey and a box are in a cage, and some bananas are hanging from the ceiling too high for the monkey to reach: How can he get them? The obvious answer is, push the box under the bananas, climb on the box, then reach the bananas. Ah, our protagonist objects, what if there is a string attached to the box which makes the bananas ascend when the box is moved? You didn't tell me there wasn't one, so there might have been. No, we reassure him, no string. Well then, he objects, what if the box is glued to the floor? No, no glue. What if the box rests on a microswitch which, when released, triggers poison-tipped arrows to shoot from the walls? No, no switches or arrows. To allay this man's paranoia once and for all, we tell him: Look, *everything is normal, it's just an ordinary cage and an ordinary*

---

[4] One is that, when a new time-dependent relation is added to the reasoner's repertoire of concepts, it should not be necessary to update all the action descriptions. This would make learning very difficult.

box: And he relaxes and believes the solution will work. What exactly did we tell him? What does it mean to say "everything is normal" or "ordinary box" or "everything has settled down" or "all is calm. . ."? If we could say what these meant, we would have the frame problem licked.

WHAT THE FRAME PROBLEM ISN'T

It is sometimes thought that the frame problem refers to the computational problem of managing a large collection of "frame axioms"; of efficient storage and rapid access on demand, and so forth. But this is a mistake. To be concerned with such matters is to have given up on the frame problem and conceded defeat. The frame problem is to find a better way of expressing the stability in which we live and on which the success of our everyday reasoning probably depends.

The frame problem is what is called in AI a representational problem, rather than a computational one. It is not concerned with such matters as the speed with which certain deductive searches can be undertaken, or how long it takes a robot to come to a decision, or how powerful a computer will be needed to get effective response times, or how many axioms will be needed to be stored in memory in order to get effective performance. If an angel appeared, telling us that Gödel had been a tool of the Devil, and gave us a magic computer which was an infinitely fast decision procedure for first-order logic, so that all our computational problems were solved at one stroke for ever and ever—if all this, the frame problem would still be with us, and just as much of a problem. It is concerned with what axioms to input to the machine, not with what the machine should do with them once it has them. It is a problem in applied philosophical logic.

The frame problem doesn't arise because the reasoner actually inhabits a changing world, only because it is having to reason about one. It is to do with beliefs about a changing world, not changing beliefs about a world. A completely separate and different problem—what has been called the updating or "truth-maintenance" problem—arises when the reasoner itself lives in a changing world, and has the task of keeping its beliefs up-to-date in the face of changing circumstances. Such a system finds that its axioms are liable to be changed from time to time, and it has to have ways to protect itself from inconsistency, and to realize when the support for its conclusions is no longer there.[5] There are two different times involved: the one the system is thinking about and the one it inhabits. The frame prob-

---

[5] Yet a third problem arises when the system has to draw conclusions on the basis of inadequate evidence, indulging in what is called nonmonotonic reasoning: It then has something like an internal qualification problem, where a conclusion drawn at one time can later be seen to be faulty just on the basis of further thinking, with no new input from outside.

lem is concerned with the former, the updating problem with the latter. A real live robot would of course often try to identify the two of them, a process which might be called keeping alert and aware, but even when they are identified, so that the robot is thinking about the world in which it lives, the frame, and updating, problems are quite distinct. The frame problem is not a problem for the robot, but for us, its designers: Without some way of solving or hacking around the frame problem, the robot wouldn't exist. The updating problem is a computational problem, a problem for the robot. We have to solve the frame problem in order to build the robot, but we have to build it so that it can solve its own updating problem.

To emphasize this distinction, since it is often misunderstood, one can imagine a program which has the updating problem in spades, but in which no frame problem arises at all: for example, an airline reservation system. Here, information is coming into the system from all sides and it is a major engineering task to maintain a consistent central representation in the system. But there's no frame problem. On the other hand, consider a program which has to plan a sequence of movements of a robot arm across a table crowded with objects, assembling and moving little heaps of them from place to place; but let the program have a complete description of this world and of the dynamics, etc., of the arm, so that no *new* information will ever come its way. It—or, more properly, the designer of it—has the frame problem, but the program has no updating problem.

A more delicate misunderstanding is to think that the frame problem is the problem of describing complex and intricate causal patterns in a dynamic world. That isn't the point. To an AI worker, difficulty in describing complexity is to be expected. What makes the frame problem so urgent and uncomfortable is precisely the opposite: It arises most acutely in very simple worlds where interactions are straightforward and nothing complex happens, what we might call the suburbia of causal interaction. People have no trouble at all reasoning about such domains, even very small children. They often find it hard to see what the difficulty is when the frame problem is first explained to them. It isn't obvious that there is any *need* to conclude that, say, picking up a glass doesn't make the table move. But this difficulty which people have illustrates, ironically, why it is such a real problem. The conclusions which we want to capture in our formal theories are so obvious that it is hard to see how even something as stupid as a computer program can have trouble with them. Conclusions which people make so quickly and with so little effort should follow very easily from our cognitive-modeling axioms. But they don't, even after twenty years.

Of course, if the world being described is simple ENOUGH, then the frame problem can be solved by just a few general axioms. A good example is the world inside a computer. One might almost define a computer memory to be a device which has many parts whose state can change very easily, but never spontaneously, and with no interactions whatsoever. An action in a computer memory is putting some string of bits b into some location l: the defining axiom is

$$contents(l,put(b,l,s)) = b$$

and the frame problem is solved by

IF $m = l$ THEN $contents(m,put(b,l,s)) = contents(m,s)$

This style of description, in terms of actions as functions from states to states, is indeed widely and successfully used in theoretical computer science, and no frame problem shows up. But it is a breathtaking engineering feat to create such an object, probably best appreciated by reading a history of the development of the computer. Most of the world isn't like this at all.

WAYS OF TRYING TO SOLVE THE FRAME PROBLEM

As McDermott (this volume) points out, a great deal of AI gets by without concerning itself about the frame problem. This is partly because much AI isn't trying to make programs which reason about the changing, everyday "common-sense" world. And it is also partly because even that part of AI which is (an area which has come to be called "planning", unfortunately), it is always possible to get by in a limited domain with some ad hoc solution which works well enough for the purpose. At worst, one can just put all those damn frame axioms in a special database and not make too much fuss about it.[6] This is also because much of the work on planning has been done in what are called "toy worlds," i.e., highly simplified and artificial domains, as I have complained elsewhere (Hayes, 1985). Unlike McDer-

---

[6] Another widely used and much-discussed idea is to have descriptions of actions state what should be made false as well as true in the new state, and have a general rule that, unless specifically falsified, whatever is true before the action is true afterwards. This idea—what Haugeland (this volume) calls the sleeping dog strategy—was pioneered in the STRIPS system used by the first mobile robot and later, with some elaboration, made a basic feature of the PLANNER and CONNIVER languages developed at MIT. The "blocks-world" reasoner incorporated into Winograd's famous SHRDLU language-comprehension system uses this strategy. It is surprisingly effective, but becomes unmanageably intricate unless restricted to very simple patterns of "deletion" in more complex domains. In any case, it doesn't really come to grips with the problem. Typically, the axiomatizations produced this way are "fragile," depending for their success on unstated assumptions about the domain being described, and when one attempts to extend them to slightly more complex worlds, they have to be rewritten from the ground up. This is a good sign that one has not managed to capture an important generalization.

mott, however, I don't think the frame problem is unreal or insignificant: It seems to point up a basic error in the way we try to describe the everyday world. We aren't carving up nature at the right ontological joints, if you ask me. But time will tell.

The basic ontology of time-instants (states, temporally possible worlds, etc.) makes no assumptions of stability whatsoever. Once a relation or term is given a temporal parameter, there is no *logical* reason why it might not change wildly in value at every moment. Indiana Jones could use this ontological framework for thinking about mine exploration: A world of explosions and booby traps fits just as cleanly into it as our more mundane world does; so of course it is no wonder that the stability which we want has to be explicitly stated somehow in our axiomatic theory. But surely, one feels, there should be some general principles which can be used to infer that moving around in a building doesn't change the color of the walls or the motions of the cars in the street.

Several attempts have been made to find such coherent and plausible principles. The first, from which the problem gets its name, was to distinguish between various "frames of reference", i.e., partitions of the set of concepts into categories enabling one to state, for example, that no action of movement affects any property of color (McCarthy & Hayes, 1969). This crude device is now usually absorbed into the more sophisticated sortal structures which are used in representational languages. Another was an attempt to explicitly state causal relationships, so that one could infer that only facts "causally connected" to an action could be affected by it (Hayes, 1971). This rapidly gets unmanageably complex, however, since one of the things which actions can do is alter the pattern of causal connections, which must themselves, therefore, be state dependent; now one has a recursive frame problem, unfortunately. In unpublished work, McCarthy is using his "circumscription" inference framework to create axiom sets which reason directly about the presence or absence of obstacles to the normal course of events. It is too early to evaluate how successful this will be.

Many people have thought that the basic ontological framework of states or time-instants is probably a mistake, for this and other reasons. It is one thing to think this, however, and another to replace it with something better. Several recent attempts center around using intervals or pieces of spacetime rather than time-instants. In these ontologies, rather than talk of a fact being true at an instant, one defines relations between connected pieces of spacetime, called "histories." For example, a cup's being on a table is described as the ON relation holding between two histories, one a temporal piece —an episode— of the whole history of the cup, the other a similar (and contemporary) episode of the history of the table. This ON relation is timeless, as indeed is the entire language, so the reasoning process bears no simple relationship to what "facts" are true at what instants. The frame problem as usually defined just doesn't crop up here, since there aren't any states or state-to-state functions in the language. The basic difficulty appears in a different guise; how to describe the possible episodes in such a way that one can conclude fairly quickly where their edges are. While it is probably too early yet to judge whether or not these ideas will be wholly successful, they illustrate again why the frame problem isn't the same as the updating problem.

My own opinion is that *the* frame problem is in fact several problems, and these might have different solutions. If you pick up a cup from a table, lots of things don't happen: The cup doesn't break, the table doesn't move, the walls don't move, your hair doesn't change color, and Jerry Fodor's refrigerator door doesn't move; or rather, if any of these things happen, it's not because of your picking up the cup. Now the cup *might* break—it depends how rough you are with it; but your hair couldn't change color— that's impossible; it's just not the kind of thing which movements cause —except perhaps in truly extraordinary circumstances, which it would usually be sensible to ignore. And the table doesn't move because it's so much heavier than the cup. (It would take a bigger shove; but only something more than a shove, something which would need tools or explosives, could move the walls.) And of course Fodor's refrigerator is just too far away to be influenced by such a small action. Each negative conclusion about a possible change is reached from a different way of thinking: Some have to do with chains of causality and barriers to it (distance, physical boundaries), some with amounts of energy and strength of materials, some with relative weights, and some follow from broad classifications of types of property and action. I suspect we have something like a Sears catalog of such stuff in our heads, a rich elaborate collection of little theories, interacting where necessary but often capable of coming to firm conclusions on the basis of beliefs about the lack of causal paths from one part of the world to another.

ON BEING PRECISE

As noted earlier, several of the papers in this volume use the term "frame problem" to refer to several different, usually more vaguely defined, problems. In several cases this seems to be something like the problem of getting a machine to reason sensibly about the world, what might be called the Generalised AI Problem, or GAIP. Sometimes it seems to be something like the general representation problem, sometimes the general control, or theorem-proving, problem. Now, the trouble with all of these discussions is that none of these "problems" is a really a problem in a technical sense. There will never be a solution to any of these "problems" because they aren't well-defined enough to have a solution. They are in the same category as the general bridge-lengthening problem (which is how to build longer bridges) or the problem of making better plastics or the problem of improving international relations. These aren't problems—they are areas of study. Of course we won't suddenly discover the answer to the GAIP, and to criticize the field because it hasn't solved it is simply to misunderstand the nature of research.

This confusion over names is especially unfortunate because, indeed, the GAIP is a very hard problem—that is, a tough research area—and progress is slow. But we have made a start, and one of the signs of some limited progress is that we are now able to make some fairly clear distinctions between distinct subproblems. We started with the GAIP, dazzled by its enormity, and now things are a bit clearer. These distinctions represent a lot of hard work, and to blur them all back into the GAIP again is a step backwards, not forwards. It would be especially regrettable if a fairly precise term such as "frame problem" became hopelessly covered in garbage as a result of its being misused by such an eminent authority as Jerry Fodor.

Fodor (this volume) makes so many mistakes that it would be improper to let them go uncorrected. His paper was inspired by his irritation at McDermott's reference (this volume) to the "sleeping-dog" strategy as being a practical solution to the frame problem, and he lets his irritation show. It will be a pleasure to respond in kind. Candor requires, for example, that I report to you the following: Fodor doesn't know the frame problem from a bunch of bananas. This is probably why he misunderstood what McDermott was saying.

Fodor misuses the term "frame problem" in at least three different ways. At first, he characterizes the frame problem as "Hamlet's problem," which as far as I can tell is something like the problem of when to stop thinking and come to a decision. If this means anything, it must be something like what I characterized above as the control, or theorem-proving, problem, although it doesn't seem to be quite that. (It's not quite clear to me that AI systems actually have this problem, in any well-defined way: It seems rather like saying they are sometimes too slow.) But in any case, whatever it is, it's certainly to do with computational matters rather than representational ones, so it isn't the frame problem. In the next paragraph, he describes it as the updating problem. Later, however, Fodor seems to characterize the frame problem as the problem of deciding what should be in the reasoner's theory, what was called above the representational problem. Well, certainly, the frame problem is part of that: Specifically, it's a problem which comes up within one particular ontological framework for describing one particular kind of world. But it's not the whole, general Problem of Representation, the whole ball of wax. If it were, of course Fodor would be right to ridicule the "sleeping-dog" strategy as a proposed solution; but it isn't, so he isn't. And certainly, these three problems aren't the same as one another. (Of course, they are all interrelated in many ways; perhaps Fodor's discussion is not meant to be taken this precisely.

But then all he is saying is something like: Gee, AI is really hard. We don't need to work with philosophers to know that, thanks.) Finally, according to Fodor, the frame problem is "just the problem of nondemonstrative inference," which is ". . . the problem of how the cognitive mind works": the GAIP again. Back to the drawing board.

Two facts are clear: Fodor is confusing or deliberately blurring several distinct problems; and whatever he means by "frame problem" is something much more general than the frame problem. Let us call this Fodor's problem, or the **fp** for brevity. I *think* it's the GAIP, but one cannot be exactly sure.

It is worth pointing out that Fodor uses a strategy of argument in this paper which *forces* the problems to be general ones. Consider, he says, an automatic scientist: His reasoning problems wouldn't involve actions necessarily, so the **fp** can't be only concerned with actions. On the other hand, a reasoner which was a mundane robot getting about *would* have to think about the effects of its actions, so the **fp** includes that case as well. It is easy to see that since reasoning can be about anything, the **fp** must be a VERY general problem. This seems to assume that there is a central talent called "reasoning" which is used in all these various cases, and which we are trying to investigate. Now, if one insists that whatever is being investigated is the same in every conceivable case, then of course each case must be a case of that thing, and it must be something very general. But this is a circular argument, and exactly how *not* to do science. Faced with a rich variety of cases, the best strategy is to look for structure among them, to distinguish differences, classify, find regularities; not to insist both that they all display the same phenomenon and that it is so deeply hidden as to be beyond our understanding. Perhaps different domains of thinking or different kinds of inferential task require different methods and strategies; in fact, this is almost certainly true. Much of our knowledge seems to be about the processes of inference making themselves: when to work rapidly, what kind of concepts are useful for what kinds of problem, when to suspect a blind alley and check one's progress critically, when to seek analogies. The relationship of this "metaknowledge" to the deductive apparatus of a reasoner, and to the ordinary axioms which describe the domain, are complex and not fully understood, but it seems clear that it is a necessary part of a powerful reasoner, natural or artificial: And this alone means that talk of the general "problem of nondemonstrative inference" is somewhat empty.

A central point in Fodor's paper is that if one chooses silly predicates and relations ("fridgeons") to be the vocabulary of one's representation, it gets to be impossible to write down sensible axioms. Put another way, it is important to design the representation, which the reasoner will use, very carefully. True. Did anyone ever think otherwise? This is exactly what AI has been emphasizing for nearly a quarter of a century (McCarthy, 1959; Minsky, 1961). As Fodor says, ". . . When we have a rigorous account of

our commonsense estimate of the world's taxonomic structure, and a notation to express it in, most of cognitive science will be finished." Well, actually, that still leaves quite a bit to do: Just the NOTATION isn't enough,
as explained below; but yup, there's a lot of truth in that. (That's exactly
why we AI folk are trying to figure out what this notation might be, you
see, Jerry; because we are trying to do cognitive science. Are *you* doing
cognitive science?)[7]

Fodor's discussion of notations, kooky and kosher concepts, and deductive "apparatus" confuses several technical issues. He points out, correctly,
that any formal notation which is rich enough to express the concepts a
reasoner will need will also be able to express concepts it should probably
avoid, like fridgeons. But this fact is not as devastating as Fodor seems to
think. He seems to believe that a reasoning system is faced with a sort of
pressure to create representations of all concepts which are definable in its
notation; that because a program COULD, in some sense, define a concept, it therefore MUST define it, or at least WILL define it unless a strong
will is constructed to protect it from this crowd of kooky concepts. But this
is just nonsense; there is no such pressure on a reasoning program. Most
reasoners, indeed, work within (some notation semantically equivalent to)
first-order logic, where new concepts are *never* defined during the ordinary inferential processes.[8]

---

[7] It may be that Fodor's point is actually a little keener: He isn't just saying that we need
to design representations carefully, he is saying that we need to come up with philosophical
principles to justify our designs. It's not enough to have the programs reasoning about blocks
on the table or cups of tea in the morning; there have to be GOOD REASONS why we chose
their ontologies the way we did. That's where the philosophy comes in; that's why we would
have to solve the problem of induction (a real bitch, that one) before our robots could chat
with granny. Ah, now, this is a REAL mistake. The philosophical problem of induction is to
find philosophically adequate justifications for the inductive processes people use, not to discover what they are. Why is Goodman's grue/bleen paradox a real philosophical problem?
Because there's no special philosophical justification for the choice of blue/green over grue/
bleen. But there are plenty of pragmatic reasons, if you are trying to incorporate these concepts in a reasoner. (Bear in mind that you would have to connect grue and bleen to the retinal
cone transducers as well. . .) But in any case, we AI hackers don't have to give any particular
philosophical justification for our choice of representational vocabulary. We will use what
works, and we will find out, ultimately, by computational experimentation. We might build a
complete working robot, induction and all, without making a scratch on the philosophical
problem of induction: that's not our business. We wouldn't need to solve the philosophical
problem of other minds in order to build a conversational program, or the problem of the *ding
an sich* in order to build a vison system, either.

[8] Higher order logical frameworks do face a problem of this kind, since there is an inference
rule—essentially the operation of lambda-abstraction—which helps to define their search space
and which can be looked at as the formation of a new concept from its definition. AI has been
aware since the mid-1960's of methods of coping with this combinatorial maze. Very simple,
standard methods will give a program the power to avoid such nonsense as fridgeons. Boyer and
Moore (1979) and Lenat (1977) provide good examples of the current state of the art, expressed in
somewhat different styles. It's not at all trivial, but it's also not impossible; it's a particularly
tricky kind of search problem.

Fodor uses the terms "notation" and "apparatus" interchangeably, without saying exactly what he means by either. There is at least a three-way distinction to be made in any careful discussion of these issues: (a) between the representational formalism or language, (b) the set of rules or interpretative mechanism which is embodied in a system, and (c) the particular beliefs which the system has at any moment.[9] By "notation", Fodor seems to mean something like the language together with the collection of primitive symbols which are the vocabulary of the beliefs. Now, *of course,* there will never be a notation, in this sense, which has the miraculous property that only cognitively useful concepts can be expressed in it: a notation whose very grammar distinguishes between kosher and kooky concepts. But the rest of the "apparatus"—notably, the interpreter—can make such distinctions, using both global structural properties of the set of beliefs and direct advice in the form of beliefs about the relevance of other beliefs.[10] It is not clear to what extent we will be able to find computational criteria which can identify interesting concepts: But, as McDermott (this volume) remarks, we certainly don't have any other way to do it.[11]

These distincions also bear on Fodor's first point, about encapsulation. Fodor (1983) defines a cognitive faculty to be "informationally encapsulated" when it does not have access to all of the information available to the whole organism, AND when this restriction is due to "...relatively unlabile, architectural features of mental organization." Let me call such faculties *architecturally* informationally encapsulated. As he points out, it seems likely that the early stages of our perceptual systems are arranged thus. (In fact, it is hard to see how they could be otherwise, in some suffi-

---

[9] Several other distinctions are also important, for example: between the syntax of the representational language and its semantics; between the inference rules which are valid and the particular inferential patterns which the interpreter generates at any moment (the search space and the control pattern); between those beliefs which are about the external world and those which are about the process of inference making itself; between various different ways the interpreter's behavior might be affected by the syntax of beliefs; between different *kinds* of representational syntax; between the syntax and how it is encoded in the computer's architecture; . . .

[10] In fact, what it chiefly needs to do is to be VERY conservative in its strategy for allowing new concepts to be defined: Let them into the vocabulary only under extreme duress, as for example if their use allows an appreciable body of the existing-belief corpus to be rewritten more compactly, or if a large number of facts about them very quickly become evident. The "apparatus" in modern deductive programs is getting very intricate, especially in systems which store and use meta-information during the deductive process itself.

[11] Of course, this apparatus can only make use of the form of the representations, as Fodor never tires of explaining to us; so in a rather abstract sense the whole system, deductive strategy and all, might be said to constitute an extended "grammar" of a notation, defined now as the set of sentences which the system as a whole will in fact generate during its deductive processes. Since the system is a machine, this set must indeed have a characterization as the language generated by a finite automaton—just formalize the structure of the whole computer, its initial memory state, etc. But this is just a computational platitude: Such a description will bear no useful relationship to the syntax of the representational language or to the interesting computational structure of the system (see Pylyshyn, 1984, for a full discussion).

ciently strict sense of "early stage," since the very edges of our perceptual systems must be driven by the direct physical energies locally impinging on them.) But reasoning—rational thought—is not informationally encapsulated, Fodor argues, since any belief MIGHT be relevant to any conclusion. Even if this is true, however, it does not follow that a rational reasoner's set of beliefs is completely shapeless. The only alternative to encapsulation is not a buzzing, blooming confusion.

Collections of formalized beliefs have a very rich structure: many kinds of structure, in fact. Concepts form elaborate hierarchies, with even more elaborate relationships to the relations which hold between them. The whole data base of beliefs can be compiled into a network of facts (NOT a semantic network, but a "connection graph"), links in which represent possible inferences (this alone reduces the search problem by several orders of magnitude), and this network is not uniformly dense, but has clusters which correspond to what are sometimes called "micro-theories." The collection of beliefs can be viewed as a set of sentences, or as a collection of "frames" (nothing to do with the frame problem), each representing an individual thing or class of things, and these two structures complement and reinforce one another. All of this can be—must be—used by the interpreter to help find its way around. And there is even a certain amount of encapsulation, it seems. Not architectural encapsulation, but real informational isolation nevertheless. We do seem to have quick, dirty deductive strategies tailored for particular topics, and they sometimes go wrong in just the way one might expect. Examples include information about time and temporal relationships, and similarly about geometric information. If our beliefs were all connected to most of the others, we would really have Hamlet's problem. But they don't seem to be: there are a lot of them, to be sure, but they are fairly sparsely connected to one another, and sometimes they explicitly claim that there isn't any connection between some of the others. For example, I believe that the positions of the planets has nothing whatever to do with what I will eat for lunch tomorrow. You don't need to do psychological experiments on me to discover this: I can tell you directly. This belief of mine might be wrong, but it certainly saves me from wasting a lot of time with a telescope when I'm hungry, or even wasting time thinking about a telescope. Enough beliefs of this kind, suitably used by the interpreter, can provide just the kind of informational isolation on which deductive efficiency probably does rely. To repeat, it's not architectural informational encapsulation, since it has been inferred from beliefs, and might be broken if my beliefs about what is relevant to what were to change. But it serves the purpose very well. (*This* Sears catalog of beliefs is distinct from the one about lack of causal connections. That one enables the deducer to decide that one event or action has no influence on some part of the external world. This catalog enables it to decide not to think about some topic any more. There could be many connections between them, as when one of the former is the reason for believing one of the latter, but they are quite distinct.)

Elsewhere Fodor refers to Hume's problem, of identifying "natural" (as opposed to "philosophical") relations. These are, of course, the primitive symbols of the system's axiomatized beliefs. Fodor is quite correct here: AI is indeed trying to locate these Humean relations. Hume thought there were only a few of them, and that was a mistake—one repeated more recently by Schank and by Wilks (they are nowadays called "semantic primitives"). In fact, there are probably, I would guess, about 5 to 10 thousand of them (Hayes, 1985). In his characteristic way, Fodor simply asserts that "we" have no idea what these relations might be. Well, again, the answer from AI is that we are working on it, and we have got somewhere, but there's a long way to go.

What then is Fodor's point in this paper? The fp—remember, he means the GAIP—is too important to be left to the hackers. To whom, then shall we entrust it? To philosophers who have made no progress on it in 2,000 years? Or is it wrong to think of making progress on it, to investigate special cases of it, to carefully distinguish subproblems, to experiment, to come up with ideas and test them; in a word, to do science? Should we rather stand in mute awe, overwhelmed by its depth and beauty?

Perhaps we should just think *very hard* and try to come up with GENERAL PRINCIPLES OF COGNITION AND INFERENCE, using our insight and understanding, but without actually *doing* anything. Now, there is a way to make a fool of yourself working separately.

REFERENCES

Boyer, R.S., & Moore, J.S. (1979). *A computational logic.* New York: Academic Press.

Fodor, J. (1983). *The modularity of mind: An essay on faculty psychology.* Cambridge, MA: MIT Press, A Bradford Book.

Hayes, P.J. (1985). The second naive physics manifest. In J. Hobbs & R. Moore (Eds.), *Formal theories of the commonsense world* (pp. 1–36). Norwood, NJ: Ablex.

Lenat, D.B. (1977). The ubiquity of discovery. *Artificial Intelligence, 9,* 257–286.

McCarthy, J. (1959). *Programs with common sense. Mechanisation of thought processes* (Vol. 1). London: Her Majesty's Stationery Office.

McCarthy, J., & Hayes, P.J. (1969). Some philosophical problems from the standpoint of artificial intelligence. In B. Meltzer & D. Michie (Eds.), *Machine Intelligence 4.* Edinburgh, Scotland: Edinburgh University Press.

Minksy, M. (1961). Steps towards artificial intelligence. *Proceedings of the Institute of Radio Engineers, 49,* 8–30.

Pylyshyn, Z. (1984). *Computation and cognition: Toward a foundation for cognitive science.* Cambridge, MA: MIT Press, A Bradford Book.

CHAPTER 8

Modules, Frames, Fridgeons, Sleeping Dogs, and the Music of the Spheres

Jerry A. Fodor

Massachusetts Institute of Technology

There are, it seems to me, two interesting ideas about modularity. The first is the idea that some of our cognitive faculties are modular. The second is the idea that some of our cognitive faculties are not.

By a modular cognitive faculty I mean—for present purposes—one that is 'informationally encapsulated'. By an informationally encapsulated cognitive faculty, I mean one that has access, in the course of its computations, to less than all of the information at the disposal of the organism whose cognitive faculty it is. So, for example, I think that the persistence of the Muller-Lyer illusion in spite of one's knowledge that it *is* an illusion strongly suggests that some of the cognitive mechanisms that mediate visual size perception must be informationally encapsulated. You know perfectly well that the lines are the same length, yet it continues to appear to you that they are not. It would seem to follow that some of what you known perfectly well is inaccessible to the cognitive mechanisms that are determining the appearances. If this is the right diagnosis, then it follows that some of those mechanisms are informationally encapsulated.

It's worth emphasizing a sense in which modular cognitive processing is *ipso facto* irrational. After all, by definition modular processing means arriving at conclusions by attending to less than all of the evidence that is relevant and available. And ignoring relevant and available evidence is, notoriously, a technique of belief fixation that will get you into trouble in the long run. Informational encapsulation is economical; it buys speed and the reduction of computational load by, in effect, drastically delimiting the database that's brought to bear in problem solving. But the price of economy is warrant. The more encapsulated the cognitive mechanisms that mediate the fixation of your beliefs, the worse is your evidence for the beliefs that you have. And, barring skeptical worries of a boring, philosophical sort, the worse your evidence for your beliefs is, the less the likelihood that your beliefs are true.

Rushing one's hurdles and jumping to conclusions is, then, a characteristic pathology of irrational cognitive strategies; and this disease modular processors have in spades. That is because the evidence they consult is essentially an **arbitrary** sample of the evidence that is relevant and available. But—and there's the point I want to emphasize for present purposes —rational processes have their debilities too; they have their characteristic hang-ups **whose outbreaks are symptoms of their very rationality.** If, for example, you undertake to consider a **non**arbitrary sample of the available and relevant evidence before you opt for a belief, *you have the problem of when the evidence you have looked at is enough.* You have, that is to say, Hamlet's problem: when to stop thinking.

The frame problem is just Hamlet's problem viewed from an engineer's perspective. You want to make a device that is rational in the sense that its mechanisms of belief fixation are unencapsulated. But you also want the device you make actually to succeed in fixing a belief or two from time to time; you don't want it to hang up the way that Hamlet did. So, on the one hand, you don't want to delimit its evidence searches **arbitrarily** (as in encapsulated systems); and, on the other hand, you want these searches to come, somehow, to an end. How is this to be arranged? What is a **non**arbitrary strategy for delimiting the evidence that should be searched in rational belief fixation? I don't know how to answer this question. If I did, I'd have solved the frame problem and I'd be rich and famous.

Here's what I have argued so far: Rational mechanisms of belief fixation are *ipso facto* unencapsulated. Unencapsulated mechanisms of belief fixation are *ipso facto* nonarbitrary in their selection of the evidence that they consult. Mechanisms of belief fixation that are nonarbitrary in their selection of the evidence that they consult are *ipso facto* confronted with Hamlet's problem. And Hamlet's problem is just the frame problem formulated in blank verse. So, two conclusions:

1. The frame problem goes very deep; it goes **as** deep as the analysis of rationality.

2. Outbreaks of the frame problem are **symptoms** of rational process-
    ing; if you're looking at a system that has the frame problem, you
    can assume that it's rational at least to the extent of being unencap-
    sulated.

The second of these conclusions is one that I particularly cherish. I
used it, in *The Modularity of Mind,* as an argument against what I take to
be modularity theory gone mad: namely, the idea that modularity is the
general case; that **all** cognitive processing is informationally encapsulated.
Roughly, the argument went like this: When we look at real, honest-to-
God *perceptual* processes, we find real honest-to-God informational encapsulation. In parsing, for example, we find computational mechanism
with access only to the acoustics of the input and the body of 'background
information' that can be formulated in a certain kind of grammar. That is
why—in my view, and contrary to the received wisdom in psychology—
there are no context effects in parsing. AND IT IS ALSO WHY THERE IS
NO FRAME PROBLEM IN PARSING. The question what evidence the
parser should consult in determining the structural description of an utter-
ance is solved arbitrarily and architecturally: Only the acoustics of the
input and the grammar are ever available. Because there is no frame problem in parsing, it is one of the few cognitive processes that we have had
any serious success in understanding.

Whereas, by contrast, when we try to build a really SMART machine
—not a machine that will parse sentences or play chess, but, say, one that
will make the breakfast without burning down the house—we get the
frame problem straight off. This, I argued in *MOM*, is precisely BECAUSE
smart processes aren't modular. Being smart, being nonmodular, and
raising the frame problem all go together. That, in a nutshell, is why,
although we have machines that parse sentences and machines that play
chess, we have no machines that will make breakfast (excepting stoves).[1]
In short, that the frame problem breaks out here and there *but does not
break out everywhere* is itself an argument for differences in kind among
cognitive mechanisms. We can understand the distribution of outbreaks of
the frame problem *on the hypothesis* that it is the chronic infirmity of ra-

---

[1] Chess playing is not, of course, a perceptual process; so how come it's modular? Some
processes are modular by brute force and some are modular in the nature of things. Parsing is a
case of the former kind; there IS relevant information in the context, but the architecture of
the mind doesn't let the parser use it. Chess playing, by contrast, is modular in the sense that
only a very restricted body of background information (call it 'chess theory') is relevant to rational play *even in principle.* This second kind of modularity, precisely because it stems from
the nature of the task rather than the architecture of the mind, isn't of much *theoretical* interest. It's interesting to the engineer, however, since informational encapsulation makes for
feasible simulation regardless of what the source of the encapsulation may be.

tional—hence unencapsulated; hence *non*modular—cognitive systems. Or so I argued in *MOM*. And so I am prepared to argue still.

Candor requires, however, that I report to you the following: This understanding of the frame problem is not universally shared. In AI, especially, the frame problem is widely viewed as a sort of a glitch, for which heuristic processing is the appropriate patch. (The technical vocabulary deployed by analysts of the frame problem has become markedly less lovely since Shakespeare discussed it in Hamlet). How could this be so? How could the depth, beauty, and urgency of the frame problem have been so widely misperceived? That, really, is what this paper is about.

What I'm inclined to think is this: The frame problem is so ubiquitous, so polymorphous, and so intimately connected with every aspect of the attempt to understand rational nondemonstrative inference, that is it quite possible for a practitioner to fail to notice when it is indeed the frame problem that he's working on. It's like the ancient doctrine about the music of spheres: If you can't hear it, that's because it's **everywhere**. Which would be OK except that if you are unable to recognize the frame problem when as a matter of fact you are having it, you may suppose that you have solved the frame problem when as a matter of fact you are begging it. Much of the history of the frame problem in AI strikes me as having that character; the discussion that follows concerns a recent and painful example.

In the paper (this volume) called, "We've Been Framed: Or, Why AI Is Innocent of the Frame Problem," Drew McDermott claims that "there is no one problem here; and hence no solution is possible or necessary." (1) The frame problem, it turns out, is a phantom that philosophers have unwittingly conjured up by making a variety of mistakes that McDermott details and undertakes to rectify.

What philosophers particularly fail to realize, according to McDermott, is that, though no solution of the frame problem is "possible or necessary," nevertheless a solution is up and running in AI. (One wonders how many other impossible and unnecessary problems McDermott and his colleagues have recently solved.) "In all systems since [1969]. . . programs have used the. . . "sleeping dog" strategy. They keep track of each situation as a separate data base. To reason about result(s,e) (i.e., about the result of an event in a situation), they compute all the effects of e in situation s, make those changes, and leave the rest of s (the 'sleeping dogs') alone." In consequence of the discovery of this sleeping dog solution, "since 1970. . . *no working AI program has ever been bothered at all by the frame problem*" (emphasis McDermott's).

It is, moreover, no accident that the sleeping dog strategy works. For it is supported by a deep metaphysical truth, namely that "most events leave most facts untouched." (2) You can rely on metaphysical inertia to carry most of the facts along from one event to the next; being carried along in this way is, as you might say, the unmarked case for facts. Because this is so, you'll usually do alright if you leave well enough alone when you update your database. Given *metaphysical* inertia, the appropriate *epistemic* strategy is to assume that nothing changes unless you have a special reason for changing it. Sleeping dogs don't scratch where it doesn't itch.

So doesn't the 'sleeping dog strategy' solve the frame problem? No. What it does is to convert the frame problem FROM A PROBLEM ABOUT BELIEF FIXATION INTO A PROBLEM ABOUT ONTOLOGY (or, what comes to much the same thing for present purposes, from a problem about belief fixation into a problem about canonical notation). This wants some spelling out.

As we've seen, the sleeping dog strategy depends on assuming that most of the facts don't change from one event to the next. And the trouble with that assumption is that WHETHER IT'S TRUE DEPENDS ON HOW YOU INDIVIDUATE FACTS. Or, to put it a little more in the formal mode, if you want to use a sleeping dog algorithm to update your database, you must first devise a system of canonical representation for the facts; (algorithms—of course—work on facts AS REPRESENTED.) And this system of canonical representation will have to have the following properties:

1. It has to be rich enough to represent all of the facts that you propose to specify in the database;
2. THE CANONICAL REPRESENTATIONS of most of the facts must be unchanged by most events. By definition, a sleeping dog algorithm *won't work* unless the canonical notation does have this second property.

The problem is—indeed, the *frame* problem is—that such notations are a little hard to come by. Oh yes, indeed they are!

Consider, for example, the following outbreak of the frame problem:

It has got to work out on any acceptable model that when I turn the refrigerator on, certain of my beliefs about the refrigerator—and about other things, of course—become candidates for getting updated. So, for example, now that the refrigerator is on, I believe that putting the legumes in the vegetable compartment will keep them cool and crispy. (I did not believe that *before* I turned the refrigerator on because until I turned the refrigerator on I believed that the refrigerator was off. Correctly, as we may assume). Similarly, now that the refrigerator is on, I believe that when the door is opened the light in the refrigerator will go on too; and I believe that my electricity meter will run slightly faster than it did before... And so forth. On the other hand, it should also fall out of a solution of the frame problem that a lot of my beliefs—indeed, MOST of my beliefs—do NOT become candidates for updating (hence don't have to be —as it were—actively reconsidered) in consequence of my plugging in the fridge. As, for example: my belief that cats are animate, my belief that Granny was a Bulgarian, my belief that snow is white. . . and so forth. I want it that most of my beliefs do not become candidates for updating because what I primarily want of my beliefs is that they should *correspond to the facts;* and, as we've seen, metaphysical inertia guarantees me that most of the FACTS are unaffected by my turning on the fridge.

Or does it? Consider a certain relational property that physical particles have from time to time: the property of BEING A FRIDGEON. I define 'x is a fridgeon at t' as follows: *x is a fridgeon at t iff x is a particle at t and my fridge is on at t.* It is, of course, a consequence of this definition that, when I turn my fridge on, I CHANGE THE STATE OF EVERY PHYSICAL PARTICLE IN THE UNIVERSE; namely, every physical particle becomes a fridgeon. (Turning the fridge off has, of course, the reverse effect.) I take it (as does McDermott, so far as I can tell) that talk about facts is intertranslatable with talk about instantiations of properties, so when I create ever so many new fridgeons, I also create ever so many new facts. The point is, of course, that if you count all these facts about fridgeons, the principle of metaphysical inertia no longer holds even of such homely events as my turning on the fridge. Or, to put the same point less metaphysically and more computationally: If I let the facts about fridgeons into my database (along with the facts about the crisping compartment and the facts about Granny's ethnic affiliations), *pursuing the sleeping dog strategy will no longer solve the frame problem.* Because: The sleeping dog strategy proposes to keep the computational load down by considering as candidates for updating only representations of such facts as an event changes. But now there are BILLIONS of facts that change when I plug in the fridge; one fact for each particle, more or less. And, of course, there's nothing special about the property of being a fridgeon; it's a triviality to think up as many more such kooky properties as you like.

I repeat the moral: Once you let representations of the kooky properties into the database, a strategy which says 'look just at the facts that change' will buy you nothing; it will commit you to looking at indefinitely many facts.

The moral was not, please notice, that the sleeping dog strategy is WRONG; it's that the sleeping dog strategy is EMPTY unless we have, together with the strategy, some idea of what is to count as a fact for the purposes at hand. Moreover, this notion—of, as we might call it, a COMPUTATIONALLY RELEVANT fact— will have to be FORMALIZED if we propose to implement the sleeping dog strategy as a computational algorithm. For, algorithms act on facts only as represented, and only in virtue of the form of their representations. So, if we want to keep the kooky facts out of the data base, and keep the computationally relevant facts in, we will have to find a way of distinguishing kooky facts from computationally relevant ones IN VIRTUE OF THE FORM OF THEIR CANONICAL REPRESENTATIONS. The frame problem, in its current guise, is the problem of formalizing this distinction. And, of course, we don't *know* how to formalize it. For that matter,—'formalize' my Bulgarian grandmother—we don't even know how to draw it!

For example, the following ways of drawing it—or of getting out of drawing it—it will quite clearly NOT work:

a. Being a fridgeon is a relational property; rule it out on those grounds.
   • Answer: Being a father is a relational property too; but we want to be able to come to believe that John is a father when we come to believe that his wife has had a child.
b. 'Fridgeon' is a made-up word. There is no such word as 'fridgeon' in English.
   • Answer: You can't rely on the lexicon of English to solve your metaphysical problems for you. There used to be no such word as 'meson' either. Moreover, though there is no such word as 'fridgeon', the expression 'x is a particle at t and my fridge is on at t' is perfectly well formed. Since this expression is the DEFINITION of 'fridgeon', everything that can be said in English by using 'fridgeon' can also be said in English without using it.
c. Being a fridgeon isn't a real property.
   • Answer: I'll be damned if I see why not, but have it your way. The frame problem is now the problem of saying what a 'real property' is.
d. Nobody actually has concepts like 'fridgeon'; so you don't have to worry about such concepts when you build your model of the mind.
   • Answer: This is another way of begging the frame problem; another way of mistaking a formulation of the problem for its solution.

     Everybody has, of course, an infinity of concepts (corresponding, roughly, to the open sentences of English). According to all known theories, the way a person keeps an infinity of concepts in a finite head is this: He stores a finite primitive basis and a finite compositional mechanism, and the recursive application of the latter to the former specifies the infinite conceptual repertoire. The present problem is that there are arbitrarily many kooky concepts—like fridgeon—which can be defined WITH THE SAME APPARATUS THAT YOU USE TO DEFINE PERFECTLY KOSHER CONCEPTS LIKE, SAY 'VEGETABLE CRISPER' OR 'BULGARIAN GRANDMOTHER'. That is, the same basic concepts that I used to define 'fridgeon', and the same logical syntax, are needed to define non-kooky concepts that people actually do entertain. So the problem—viz. the FRAME problem—is to find a RULE that will keep the kooky concepts out while letting the non-kooky concepts in.

I remind you that, lacking a solution to this problem, YOU CANNOT IMPLEMENT A SLEEPING DOG 'SOLUTION' TO THE FRAME PROBLEM; it will not run. It will not run because, at each event, it will be required to update indefinitely many beliefs about the distribution of kooky properties.

e. But McDermott says that solutions to the frame problem have actually been implemented; that nobody in AI has had to worry about the frame problem since way back in '69. So something MUST be wrong with your argument.

- Answer: the programs run because the counterexamples are not allowed to arise. The programmer decides what kinds of properties get specified in the database, but the decision is unsystematic and unprincipled. For example, no database will be allowed to include information about the distribution of fridgeons; but, as we've seen, there appears to be no disciplined way to justify the exclusion and no way to implement it that doesn't involve excluding indefinitely many computationally relevant concepts as well.

There is, of course, a price to be paid for not facing the frame problem. The conceptual repertoires with which AI systems are allowed to operate exclude kooky and kosher concepts indiscriminately. They are therefore grossly impoverished in comparison with the conceptual repertoires of really intelligent systems like you and me. The consequence (one of the worst-kept secrets in the world, I should think) is that these artificially intelligent systems—the ones that have been running since 1970 "without ever being bothered by the frame problem" you know? —are, by any reasonable standards, ludicrously stupid.

You may be beginning to wonder what is actually going on here. Well, because the frame problem is just the problem of nondemonstrative inference, a good way to see what is actually going on is to think about how the 'sleeping dog' strategy works when it's applied to confirmation in science; our best case of the systematic pursuit of knowledge through nondemonstrative inference, as I have repeatedly remarked.

Looked at from this perspective, the sleeping dog strategy is precisely analogous to a principle of scientific 'conservatism'; that is, to a principle which says 'alter the MINIMUM possible amount of prior theory when you go about accommodating new data'. Notice, however, that while it is widely agreed that conservatism, in this sense, is constitutive of rational scientific practice, the maxim as I've just stated it doesn't amount to anything like a formal principle for theory choice (just as, of course, the 'sleeping dog' strategy as McDermott states it doesn't constitute anything like a algorithm for updating databases). You could, of course, MAKE the principle of conservatism into a formal evaluation metric by specifying (a) a canonical notation for writing scientific theories and (b) a costing system (e.g., the most conservative change in a theory is the one that alters the fewest symbols in its canonical representation). Given (a) and (b), we would have an important fragment of a mechanical evaluation procedure for science. Which would be a NICE thing for us to have. So why doesn't somebody go and build us one?

Well, because not just ANY canonical notation will do the job. To do the job, you have to build a notation such that (relative to the costing system, THE (intuitively) MOST CONSERVATIVE REVISION OF A THEORY DOES INDEED COME OUT TO BE THE SIMPLEST ONE WHEN THE THEORY IS CANONICALLY REPRESENTED. (So, for example, if your accounting system says 'choose the alteration that can be specified in the smallest number of canonical symbols', then your notation has to have the property that the intuitively most conservative alteration actually does come out shortest when the theory is in canonical form). And, of course, nobody knows how to construct a notation with that agreeable property. JUST AS NOBODY KNOWS HOW TO CONSTRUCT A NOTATION FOR FACTS SUCH THAT, UNDER THAT NOTATION, MOST FACTS ARE UNCHANGED BY MOST EVENTS.

It isn't, of course, surprising that such notations don't grow on trees. If somebody developed a vocabulary for writing scientific theories which had the property that the shortest description of the world in that vocabulary was always the best theory of the world available, that would mean that the notation gave FORMAL EXPRESSION to our most favored inductive estimate of the world's taxonomic structure. Well, when we have an inductive estimate of the world's taxonomic structure that's good enough to permit formal expression, and a canonical vocabulary to formulate the taxonomy in, most of science will be finished.

Similarly, *mutatis mutandis,* in cognitive theory. A notation adequate to support an implemented sleeping dog algorithm would be one which represents as facts only what we commonsensically take to really *be* facts: the ethnicity of grandmothers; the situation, temperature-wise, in the vegetable crisper; but not the current distribution of fridgeons. In effect, the notation would give formal expression to our *commonsense* estimate of the world's taxonomic structure. Well, when we have a rigorous account of our commonsense estimate of the world's taxonomic structure, and a notation to express it in, most of *cognitive* science will be finished.

In short, there is no formal conservatism principle for science for much the same sort of reason that there is no workable sleeping dog algorithm. Basically, the solution of both problems requires a notation which formalizes our intuitions about inductive relevance. There is, however, the following asymmetry: We can do science perfectly well without having a formal theory of nondemonstrative inference; which is to say that we can do science perfectly well without solving the frame problem. That's because doing science doesn't require having *mechanical* scientists; we have *us* instead. But we can't do AI perfectly well without having mechanical intelligence; doing AI perfectly well just *is* having mechanical intelligence. So we can't do AI without solving the frame problem. But *we don't know how* to solve the frame problem. That, in a nutshell, is why, though science works, AI doesn't.

I reiterate the main point: The frame problem and the problem of formalizing our intuitions about inductive relevance are, in every important respect, THE SAME THING. It is just as well, perhaps, that people working on the frame problem in AI are unaware that this is so. One imagines the expression of horror that flickers across their CRT-illuminated faces as the awful facts sink in. What could they do but down tools and become *philosophers*? One feels for them. Just *think* of the cut in pay!

God, according to Einstein, does not play dice with the world. Well, maybe; but He sure is into shell games. If you do not understand the logical geography of the frame problem, you will only succeed in pushing it around from one shell to the next, never locating it for long enough to have a chance of solving it. This is, so far as I can see, pretty much the history of the frame problem in AI; which is a main reason why AI work, when viewed as cognitive theory, strikes one as so *thin*. The frame problem—to say it one last time—is just the problem of nondemonstrative inference; and the problem of nondemonstrative inference is—to all intents and purposes—the problem of how the cognitive mind works. I am sorry that McDermott is out of temper with philosophers; but, frankly, the frame problem is too important to leave it to the hackers.

Look guys, we are really going to have to learn to make progress working together; the alternative is to make fools of ourselves working separately.

POSTSCRIPT

Elsewhere in this volume Pat Hayes thrashes about for a reply to this indictment, but as far as I can tell, he gets nowhere beyond insisting upon a terminology that segregates a galaxy of problems which—if my arguments are right—MUST be solved together if they are to be solved at all.

There is, however, one mistake of Hayes' which is central and egregious. He remarks (vis-à-vis the fridgeon problem) that I "seem to believe that a reasoning system is faced with a sort of pressure to create representations of all concepts which are definable in its notation; that because a program COULD, in some sense, define a concept, it therefore MUST define it..." and so forth.

Now, the precise sense in which a program with access to the concepts 'refrigerator', 'particle'...etc. and the logical connectives COULD define 'fridgeon' is patent; in fact, I gave the definition. So the problem is to say **what stops it from doing so?** That it isn't **forced** to create the concept is true but utterly irrelevant; it isn't FORCED to create the concept 'chair' either. The point is that it's **equipped** to do so (in both cases) and that *if* it does so it will thereby be enabled to think true thoughts (again in both cases; for there really are fridgeons, just as there really are chairs).

Strictly speaking, by the way, I don't like this talk of 'creating concepts'. The point is that the robot's database will specify certain properties of its world and won't specify others. *Ceteris paribus*, we want it to specify the distribution of chairs but not the distribution of fridgeons; and the problem is that we don't know how to bring this about. That problem MUST be solved because, if it's not, sleeping dog algorithms won't work. I agree with Hayes that, if you don't call this the frame problem, that makes what you do call the frame problem easier. What I don't understand is why Hayes finds this banal observation comforting. If you don't call it cancer, then what you do call cancer won't be what you die of. But you end up equally dead either way.

Author Index

Subject Index